A LESSON FOR EVERY DAY

LITERACY

4–5 YEARS

4–5 YEARS

A & C Black • London

Published 2010 by A & C Black Publishers Limited
36 Soho Square, London W1D 3QY
www.acblack.com
ISBN 978-1-4081-2535-9
Copyright text © Christine Moorcroft 2010
Editors: Dodi Beardshaw, Jane Klima, Marie Lister, Clare Robertson, Lynne Williamson
Compiled by Mary Nathan and Fakenham Photosetting

The authors and publishers would like to thank Ray Barker, Fleur Lawrence and Rifat Siddiqui for their advice in
producing this series of books.

Every effort has been made to trace copyright holders and obtain their permission for use of copyright material. The
publishers would be pleased to rectify any error or omission in future editions.

A CIP catalogue record for this book is available from the British Library.

Printed and bound in Great Britain by Martins the Printers, Berwick-on-Tweed.

A & C Black uses paper produced with elemental chlorine-free pulp, harvested from managed sustainable forests.

Contents

Introduction

Introduction

A Lesson for Every Day: Literacy is a series of seven photocopiable activity books for developing children's ability to communicate with others through speaking and listening, and reading and writing.

The activities provide opportunities for children to read different genres, and to read fluently through using phonic knowledge of grapheme-phoneme correspondences and blending as their prime approach for decoding unfamiliar words. The books also help children to spell words accurately by combining the use of grapheme–phoneme correspondence knowledge as the prime approach, and morphological knowledge and etymological information.

The series develops children's understanding of sentences and their ability to form sentences, with activities that help them to practise their skills in organising and writing texts for different purposes.

The importance of dance, songs and rhymes is recognised in the development of communication skills. The activities provide or are linked to various games, rhymes, songs and stories as well as to familiar or everyday situations.

The activities

To help teachers to select appropriate learning experiences for their pupils, the activities have been grouped in the sections found in the Early Years Foundation Stage area of Learning and Development 'Communication, Language and Literacy'. However, the activities need not be presented to children in the order in which they appear in the book, unless otherwise stated.

Some of the activities can be carried out with the whole class, some are more suitable for small groups and others are for individual work, especially where the teacher and teaching assistants are working more closely with

other groups. Many are generic and can be adapted; the notes on the activities in the grids on pages 6-24 and, in some cases, the notes at the foot of the page provide suggestions and ideas for this and for developing extension activities. Many of the activities can be adapted for use at different levels, to suit the differing levels of attainment of the children (see the teachers' notes on the pages). The activities can be used in connection with different areas of the curriculum, some of which are suggested in the notes on the activities.

The activities emphasise the importance of providing opportunities for children to enjoy novels, stories, plays, films and poetry – not just to learn about how they are written – and that children have time to listen to, repeat, learn, recite and join in poems for enjoyment. It is also important to encourage children to read non-fiction for enjoyment as well as for finding specific information.

Reading

Most children will be able to carry out the activities independently but some may need help in reading the instructions on the sheets. It is expected that someone will read them to or with them, since children learn to recognise the purpose of instructions before they can read them.

Organisation

The activities require very few resources besides pencils, crayons, scissors and glue. Other materials are specified in the teachers' notes on the pages: for example, story books, nursery rhymes, an interactive whiteboard, audio or video recording equipment (such as a tape recorder, camera or

mobile phone) soft toys, dressing-up items, information books and dictionaries.

Extension activities

Most of the activity sheets end with a challenge (**Now try this!**) which reinforces and extends the children's learning. These more challenging activities might be appropriate for only a few children; it is not expected that the whole class should complete them, although many more children might benefit from them with appropriate assistance – possibly as a guided or shared activity. On some pages there is space for the children to complete extension activities that involve writing or drawing, but others will require a separate sheet of paper.

Notes on the activities

The notes on the activities in the grids on pages 6-24 expand upon those which are provided at the bottom of most activity pages. They give ideas and suggestions for making the most of the activity sheet, including suggestions for the whole-class introduction, the plenary session or for follow-up work using an adapted version of the activity sheet.

Assessment

Use the completed activities as part of your day-to-day assessment to help you to build a picture of children's learning in order to plan future teaching and learning. Activities can also be used as examples of significant evidence for your periodic assessment. In order to help you to make reliable judgements about your pupils' attainment, the Early Years Foundation Stage scale points for each activity and the Assessment Focuses for Assessing Pupils' Progress are given in the grids on pages 6-24. Some of the activities provide opportunities for children to carry out self assessment. Encourage children to reflect on their learning and discuss with them whether there are areas that they feel they need to practise further.

The CD-ROM

All activity sheets can be found as PDF and Word versions on the accompanying CD-ROM. These can be printed or displayed on an interactive whiteboard. The Word versions can be customised in Microsoft Word in order to assist personalised learning.

They can be accessed through an interface that makes it easy to select worksheets and display them. You can also search for lessons that will meet a particular EYFS scale point or Assessment Focus for Assessing Pupils' Progress. For more information on system requirements, please see the inside front cover.

If you have any questions regarding the *A Lesson For Every Day* CD-ROM, please email us at the address below. We will get back to you as soon as possible.

educationalsales@acblack.com

Language for communication

Activity name	Strand and learning objectives	Notes on the activities	Assessment Focus	Page number
How could you help? Keep Grandma safe	**1. Speaking** Enjoy listening to and using spoken and written language and readily turn to it in play and learning	**How could you help?** and **Keep Grandma safe** foster enjoyment of stories and encourage the children to use spoken language in learning. You could first recite some of the nursery rhymes featured in *How could you help?* with them. Invite volunteers to choose a character and to say what problem he, she or it had: for example, being badly injured when falling down a hill, being frightened by a spider, being left with unwanted tea after making it for people who went away, losing a pocket (purse), having a lamb follow her into her classroom, falling off a wall and being injured, having their tails cut off by an angry farmer's wife, being washed down a drain, having no food for her dog, having a seriously overcrowded house, falling asleep when he was meant to be looking after the cattle and sheep – which then ruined the crops when they escaped, being thrown down a well. This could be linked with work in Citizenship (Taking part, Choices, Animals and us and People who help us). Once the children have described the problem give them time to think about (or discuss with a friend) how they could help the character to solve it or prevent it happening again or happening to others. You could help with questions such as *What does she need? What would make her happy? What would make them feel better? What help do they need?*	**EYFS Scale Point 3** **Speaking and listening AF1** Talk in purposeful and imaginative ways to explore ideas and feelings, adapting and varying structure and vocabulary according to purpose, listeners, and content	25 26
The new baby Moving house I can draw a house Phone a friend Sally go round the Sun Twinkle, twinkle little star	**1. Speaking** Speak clearly and audibly with confidence and control and show awareness of the listener	**The new baby** focuses on using talk to imagine and recreate experiences and helps to develop skills in speaking clearly and audibly. You could prepare for this by asking if anyone who has a new baby in their family would like to talk about it and give them the opportunity to bring in props to help them, such as photographs and baby items: for example, the baby's first shoes or other clothing, or a favourite toy. It might help if there is a special place for a 'speaker' to sit or stand; this could be used whenever someone speaks to the class. It could have 'buttons' or 'switches' to remind the children to 'switch on' their 'good speaking' voices and actions: Speak clearly and not too fast. Look up. Use expression. It helps if you demonstrate 'bad speaking' and ask the children what was wrong: mumble, speak too quickly, look at the ground, speak in a monotonous voice. **Vocabulary:** *baby, clearly, expression, new.* **Moving house** is about using talk to imagine and recreate experiences. It presents a setting that will be familiar for many children and which many find unsettling but others view with delight. It could help them to explore and resolve their worries or to relive an exciting event. You could record some of the children's discussions and ask them about them afterwards or invite them to talk about what they wrote in the speech bubbles. **Vocabulary:** *house, move, removal, van.* **I can draw a house** could provide the basis for the children to draw a house resembling their own or one they have seen, or a house in a story. Encourage them to use their own ideas of details to include and to choose the style of the windows and doors. **Vocabulary:** *answer, ask, goodbye, hello, invite, listen, phone, say, speak, talk, tell.* **Phone a friend** draws on the children's everyday experience of listening to adults using phones, and of using real and 'play' phones themselves. **Vocabulary:** *answer, ask, goodbye, hello, invite, listen, phone, say, speak, talk, tell.* **Sally go round the Sun.** The children could replace 'Sally' with their own name when reciting the rhyme. Praise children who are behaving as good listeners. **Vocabulary:** *learn, listen, recite, rhyme, say.* **Twinkle, twinkle, little star** can be extended as an activity by changing the last word of the first line and inviting volunteers to change the second line to make a new rhyme: for example, "Twinkle, twinkle, little bell. / How I wonder what you tell!" or "Twinkle, twinkle, little bee, / How I wonder what you see!" To develop skills in speaking with confidence, set up a mini-performance of the children's favourite rhymes. **Vocabulary:** *learn, line, nursery, record, rhyme, rhyming, say.*	**EYFS Scale Point 8** **Speaking and listening AF1** Talk in purposeful and imaginative ways to explore ideas and feelings, adapting and varying structure and vocabulary according to purpose, listeners, and content	27 28 29 30 31 32

Activity	Objectives	Description	Assessment focuses	Page
Action words Action places Sounds and words I like this word Whisky frisky: 1 and 2	**1. Speaking** **2. Listening and responding** **7. Understanding and responding to texts** Extend their vocabulary, exploring the meanings and sounds of new words	**Action words** and **Action places** help to extend the children's vocabulary and to explore the meanings and sounds of new words as they match alliterative phrases to actions and locations. You could begin with the story *We're Going on a Bear Hunt* (Michael Rosen & Helen Oxenbury, Walker Books) and let the children do the actions, perhaps on a walk in a large area such as the hall, school grounds or park. Encourage the children to join in the actions: for example, Scramble and stumble across the rocks. It could be made into a song as you do so. They could make up their own words for actions through places they encounter. Encourage them to say the words as they do the actions. **Vocabulary:** *clamber, climb, crawl, creep, crunch, dodge, duck, glide, jitter, jump, scramble, scrape, scratch, scrunch, slide, splash, swish, tumble, wobble.* **Sounds and words** helps to extend the children's vocabulary and to explore the meanings and sounds of new words as they do the animals' actions and match the animals to words for their movements. This activity also provides an opportunity for speaking clearly and audibly with confidence and control as the children say the words in a way that sounds like their meanings and the movements of the animals. They could begin by doing the actions (perhaps just using their hands). You could model the appropriate tone and speed of voice for each action. They could make up endings for others (with pictures from books as clues); for example, *I'm a busy buzzing (bee). I'm a leaping loping (kangaroo).* **Vocabulary:** *flitting, fluttering, grumbling, scrabbling, scuttling, sliding, slipping, stumbling.* **I like this word** helps to extend the children's vocabulary and explore the meanings and sounds of words. You could adapt this page to feature interesting words the children come across in stories, and build a display or collection of children's choices of favourite or interesting words. Also model how to use dictionaries to look up the meanings of words. **Vocabulary:** *avocado, ferocious, gleaming, wombat.* **Whisky frisky: 1** and **2** focus on the rhymes and sounds of words and the ways in which they rhyme (without using the technical terms): for example, the internal rhyme of 'Whisky frisky', 'Whirly twirly' and 'Furly curly'; the onomatopoeia of 'Snap! Crack!'; and the alliteration of 'Hipperty hop'. The children could recite the poem using the cut-out squirrel as a prop. **Vocabulary:** *learn, move, poem, rhyme, say, sound.*	**EYFS Scale Point 9** **Speaking and listening AF1** Talk in purposeful and imaginative ways to explore ideas and feelings, adapting and varying structure and vocabulary according to purpose, listeners, and content **Speaking and listening AF2** Listen and respond to others, including in pairs and groups, shaping meanings through suggestions, comments, and questions **Speaking and listening AF4** Understand the range and uses of spoken language, commenting on meaning and impact and draw on this when talking to others **Reading AF2** Understand, describe, select or retrieve information, events or ideas from texts and use quotation and reference to text **Reading AF3** Deduce, infer or interpret information, events or ideas from texts **Reading AF1** Use a range of strategies including accurate decoding of text, to read for meaning **Reading AF4** Identify and comment on the structure and organization of texts, including grammatical and presentational features at text level **Reading AF5** Explain and comment on writers' uses of language, including grammatical and literary features at word and sentence level	33 34 35 36 37–38

	2. Listening and responding 8. Engaging and responding to texts Listen with enjoyment and respond to stories, songs and other music, rhymes and poems and make up their own stories, songs, rhymes and poems		EYFS Scale Point 4 Speaking and listening AF2 Listen and respond to others, including in pairs and groups, shaping meanings through suggestions, comments, and questions All Reading AFs, especially: Reading AF6 Identify and comment on writers' purposes and viewpoints and the overall effect of the text on the reader Reading AF3 Deduce, infer or interpret information, events or ideas from texts Reading AF7 Relate texts to their social, cultural and historical contexts and literary traditions	
Way down south		**Way down south** is about the children listening with enjoyment to rhymes and responding to what they have heard by relevant actions. Help the children to repeat this rhyme with expression: the first three lines in a sing-song story-telling tone, with the last line emphatically – even shouted. The children could collect pictures of animals from comics, magazines or colouring books and add their own verses. You could scan these pictures and use the copy on the CD-ROM to insert them instead of the pictures provided. You might need first to draw text boxes within the chart. The activity could be linked with work in Geography (Knowledge and understanding of the world): show the children pictures of countries where bananas grow and help them to find them on a globe. You could also show them pictures of northern parts of the world (and point them out on the globe) and change the rhyme to match them, for example: *Way up north where there's always snow* *An arctic hare stood on a polar bear's toe.* *The polar bear said with tears in his eyes,* *"Pick on somebody your own size."* **Vocabulary:** *down, east, north, size, south, up, west.*		39
Merry Mr Cherry		**Merry Mr Cherry** provides an opportunity to listen to, enjoy and respond to a rhyme. It requires sustained listening in order to be able to reverse the rhyme. Children could mime/play the roles in the rhyme as they say it. Supply some names to help them (and some rhyming words, if necessary); for example, Carol O'Farrell (barrel), plain Miss Lane (train), silly Billy Tilley (filly). The activity is based on the structure of *Hairy Maclary from Donaldson's Dairy* (Lynley Dodd, Puffin), which could also be used for activities of this type. The animals in the story are described in rhyme: for example, *Hairy Maclary from Donaldson's Dairy* and *Muffin McLay like a bundle of hay.* After reading the rhyme accompanying the fourth picture, introduce a 'fright' (or ask any children who have completed the extension activity what 'fright' they have in their rhyme): for example, a wild animal chases the procession of people, beginning with the one at the back (the two Miss Tates) and then the others, in reverse order. This can be linked with mathematical development (positional language). **Vocabulary:** *along, backwards, down, forwards, fright, order, over.*		40
Under the dark		**Under the dark** helps the children to listen with enjoyment and respond to a poem. You could read it in a quiet tone of voice that suggests mystery and awe. Ask them what the poem makes them think of and how it makes them feel. With the children, you could make up actions to accompany the poem: for example, hands cupped around their eyes like binoculars for 'under the dark'; then draw a star shape in the air, use the forearms pressed close together and held vertically with hands opened out for 'a tree' then mime spreading a blanket and point to themselves for 'me'. You could also ask them to choose the most appropriate words from a list to describe it. **Vocabulary:** *calm, exciting, frightening, happy, jolly, lively, marching, poem, quiet, sad, scary, under.*		41
Story characters: listen and tell		**Story characters: listen and tell** helps the children to listen with enjoyment and respond to stories by asking them to listen to one another saying what they know about a character in the story. Ask the speaker not to let the others see the picture of the character so that they have to listen carefully. Model the language children might use, for example *This character has... lives... is a....* You could introduce variations, such as awarding three points for those who guess after the speaker has given only one piece of information, two points after two and so on. **Vocabulary:** *character.*		42
Offstage: 1		**Offstage: 1** provides support for developing the children's ability to listen with enjoyment and respond to stories by encouraging them to think about what might have been going on in a scene but is not included in the story. Here they are asked what Cinderella's father or other people in the household might have been doing or saying late at night as she ran home from the ball. You could also talk about what other people at the ball, including the ugly sisters and the prince, might have been doing and saying. **Vocabulary:** *at the same time, happen, happening.*		43
Offstage: 2		**Offstage: 2** is about listening with enjoyment and responding to stories. It encourages the children to think about what might have been going on in a scene but is not included in the story. Here they are asked to consider what the other two Billy Goats Gruff might have been doing or saying while this Billy Goat was crossing the Troll's bridge. You could also talk about what other characters might have been there (for example, the Troll's family) and what they might have been doing. **Vocabulary:** *at the same time, happen, happening.*		44
The three little pigs		**The three little pigs** is about listening with enjoyment and responding to stories. The children need to listen carefully to the story in order to sequence the pictures and then retell the story, using the pictures as prompts. Encourage them to add their own words or actions. You could link this with work in Science (Knowledge and understanding of the world) on materials and their uses. **Vocabulary:** *bricks, order, story, straw, wood.*		45
Goldilocks story maze		**Goldilocks story maze** encourages listening with enjoyment and responding to stories. The children need to listen carefully to the story to know the characters and decide whether it belongs to the story. As they move their finger along the maze they should stop at each picture and decide whether it belongs to the story. They could colour the ones that belong. Afterwards you could ask them what they know about one of the characters or objects. You could also use the CD-ROM to adapt this page to make mazes about other stories they have heard. If possible, make life-size story mazes in the hall or playground using dressed up dolls as characters and various items as props. The route could be chalked on the ground or made using barriers such as cones and ropes or canes. **Vocabulary:** *ahead, follow, left, maze, right, straight on, turn.*		46

Section / Activity	Description	EYFS Scale Point	Page
2. Listening and responding Sustain attentive listening, responding to what they have heard by relevant comments, questions or actions		**EYFS Scale Point 4** **Speaking and listening AF2** Listen and respond to others, including in pairs and groups, shaping meanings through suggestions, comments, and questions	
Partners	**Partners** is about sustaining active listening with the children, responding to what they have heard by making relevant comments or asking questions. You could remind them to look at their partners, listen to what they say and ask questions to find out more: for example, *What is your favourite colour? What does it make you think of? What food do you like best? What do you like doing?* You could even set up a video camera or use a mobile phone to record them making presentations about the others – introducing them to another class or telling their own class more about them. Download these onto a computer so that the children can play them back and watch them. Watching and listening to them could help with assessment, using page 48. **Vocabulary:** *favourite, listen.*		47
What's in the road?	**What's in the road?** and **Things in the road** are about sustaining active listening with the children, responding to what they have heard by comments and actions, listening with enjoyment and responding to rhymes. After following the suggestion in the Teachers' notes about the first verse, read the second and third verses and encourage the children to look at the pictures to help them to give Mr Toad's reply. They could then recite the fourth verse, repeating Mr Toad's previous answer and adding to it. This is a cumulative rhyme that requires the children to listen carefully, repeat what they have heard and then add to it in the correct sequence. Some of them might be able to add other vehicles: eleven, twelve, thirteen and so on... coaches, diggers, mopeds, motorbikes, scooters, steamrollers, tankers, wagons. **Vocabulary:** *along, bike, bus, car, digger, jeep, horse, lorry, tractor, truck, van.*		48
Things in the road			49
Six jolly sailors	**Six jolly sailors** is about sustaining active listening, responding to what they have heard by comments and actions and listening with enjoyment and responding to rhymes. This is a diminishing rhyme that requires the children to listen carefully, repeat what they have heard and then add to it in the correct sequence. They could make up their own version in another setting: *Six happy farmers, Six dizzy dancers.* Encourage them to think of suitable ways for these to disappear: buried alive, lost on the moor, stung by a bee, deafened by a moo, shot with a gun, danced down the drive, fell on the floor, bitten by a flea, scared by a 'boo', leapt to the sun. **Vocabulary:** *ashore, rhyme, sailor, swam, swim, verse.*		50
Mrs Topping's shopping	**Mrs Topping's shopping** is about sustaining active listening, responding to what they have heard by comments and actions. This is a cumulative story that requires the children to listen carefully, repeat what they have heard and then add to it in the correct sequence. They could add or substitute other shopping to make up their own 'story game'. You could use this activity in different ways, as suggested in the notes on the page itself or as a different kind of listening game. Give each child a card and ask the class or group to listen to what you say: for example, *On Monday Mrs Topping went shopping. She bought a hat and some gloves*, then *On Tuesday Mrs Topping went shopping. She bought some eggs, some coffee and a loaf of bread.* When the children hear what is on their card they could stand up and run around the outside of the circle and back to their places. **Vocabulary:** *list, shopping.*		51
3. Group discussion and interaction Interact with others, negotiating plans and activities and taking turns in conversation		**EYFS Scale Point 6** **Speaking and listening AF2** Listen and respond to others, including in pairs and groups, shaping meanings through suggestions, comments, and questions	
Packed lunch: 1 and 2	**Packed lunch: 1 and 2** encourage the children to use talk to clarify their thinking and to interact with others, take turns in conversation and negotiate plans as they work with a group to make choices about the lunchbox. The activity requires the children to interact and negotiate with one another. Point out that they should listen to one another. It might be necessary to model how to explain why one item should be packed in the lunchbox but not another. They should cut out the objects on page 53 and glue them into the lunchbox on page 52. This could be linked with work in Citizenship (Choices – making healthy choices). **Vocabulary:** *choose, decide, fruit, healthy, lunch, savoury, sweet.*		52–53
A day out	**A day out** focuses on using talk to clarify their thinking, interacting with others, negotiating plans and taking turns in conversation as the children work together to plan a day out. They could also take part in the planning of a real day out or a 'teddy bears' picnic'. **Vocabulary:** *choose, countryside, decide, fair, picnic, plan, railway, restaurant, seaside, train, zoo.*		54
Tell the way	**Tell the way** involves interacting and co-operating with others and using talk to sequence thinking. The children could also direct programmable toys along a track, and instruct a partner on how to get from one place in the classroom to another. Link this with work in Geography (Knowledge and understanding of the world – making simple pictorial maps to represent a short walk). **Vocabulary:** *backwards, forwards, go, left, right, stop, turn, way.*		55
Sandcastles	**Sandcastles** involves interacting with others and taking turns in conversation as the children discuss the order in which the events in the pictures took place. You could ask questions to help them: for example, *What did he do before he put the shells on the sandcastle? How could he turn the sandcastle out of the bucket with a flag on it?* This requires them to think about a familiar experience (they should first have had chances to make sandcastles in the sand tray). Some children might be able to use the sequenced pictures to give instructions for making sandcastles. **Vocabulary:** *bucket, flag, sand, sandcastle, seaside, shell, spade.*		56
The best pencil-holder	**The best pencil-holder** develops skills in interacting with others and taking turns in conversation as the children discuss the merits of the pencil-holders. Point out that it does not matter if more than one of them choose the same pencil-holder. Model phrases such as: *I think the... would be best because... But what about...? I agree that...* This could be linked with Design and technology (Creative development). **Vocabulary:** *better, best, good, pencil-case, pencil-holder.*		57
Shopping	**Shopping** focuses on using talk to clarify their thinking, interacting with others and taking turns in conversation as the children discuss what each story character might buy, and why. This will also involve talking about, and recalling, the stories. **Vocabulary:** *apple, bunch, buy, porridge, rubber gloves, shopping.*		58
That's wrong!	**That's wrong!** develops skills in interacting with others and taking turns in conversation as well as using talk to clarify thinking, as the children discuss the mistakes in the picture. **Vocabulary:** *backwards, bonnet, bumper, car, driver, forwards, headlights, sail, steering wheel, wheel, window, windscreen.*		59

Language for thinking

Activity name	Strand and learning objectives	Notes on the activities	Assessment Focus	Page number
Making things: actions	**1. Speaking** **3. Group discussion and interaction** Use talk to organise, sequence and clarify thinking, ideas, feelings and events	**Making things: actions** and **Making things: materials** provide an opportunity for using talk to sequence and clarify thinking. This page can be edited using the CD-ROM to feature items the children have made and the materials they used. You could even insert photographs along with the text. You could model a silly one for the children to correct: for example, *I made a hat with flour, sugar, eggs, butter and milk.* **Vocabulary:** *make, material.*	**EYFS Scale Point 7**	60–61
Making things: materials			**Speaking and listening AF1** Talk in purposeful and imaginative ways to explore ideas and feelings, adapting and varying structure and vocabulary according to purpose, listeners, and content	62
What's up the magic tree?		**What's up the magic tree?** encourages the children to enjoy spoken language and use talk to sequence and clarify thinking, ideas, feelings and events. Ask them how a magic tree might be different from any other tree. Once they have talked about their ideas and drawn and written them they could begin to tell a story about May and the magic tree. **Vocabulary:** *magic, tree, up.*		63
Say what you know		**Say what you know** focuses on using talk to clarify thinking and encourages them to turn to talk in learning. After they have played the game they could choose an animal they talked about, think about what they know and then consider what they do not know about it. Say what the animal is and what they know about it: for example, what it looks like, what colour it is, how big it is, whether it has legs, how many, whether it has wings, claws or a beak, where it lives, what it eats. What question would they like to answer? You could help them to find out more from information books. To help them you could ask about the animal's appearance, legs, feet, head or body covering, how it moves, where it lives, what it eats and where and how it gets its food. **Vocabulary:** *animal, body, feed, food, skin, teeth.*	**Speaking and listening AF2** Listen and respond to others, including in pairs and groups, shaping meanings through suggestions, comments, and questions	
It's a mystery		**It's a mystery** encourages the children to use talk to clarify their thinking, as they work with a partner to put the pieces into place to make a picture. Ask them how they knew which piece to put at the top and how they knew on which side to place it. It requires the children to work together. They will need to talk to one another to solve the puzzle of what is in the picture. The extension activity can be introduced to a group of four who have no difficulty with this. Introduce it in the same way. Each child has a different sentence about an animal. Ask them what it could be. Without the help of the others they cannot be certain. Another way to use this is to give each of four children one of the cards and help them to read it. If they can, invite them to read the cards aloud to another group, who could listen and say what animal they have described. **Vocabulary:** *bottom, help, left, listen, mystery, object, rabbit, right, side, slime, slimy, snail, talk, top, trail.*		64
What are they like?		**What are they like?** develops skills in using talk to clarify thinking, ideas and feelings. It could be linked with work in Citizenship (Taking part, Choices, Living in a diverse world) with a focus on making friends and knowing whom to trust. It is useful to point out that people might not be how they seem, and perhaps link this with stories such as *Beauty and the Beast* (Ladybird). **Vocabulary:** *friend, funny, grumpy, kind, lively, mean, miserable, pleasant, unkind, unpleasant.*		65
What's the story?		**What's the story?** develops skills in using talk to clarify thinking, ideas, feelings and events as the children talk to a friend about what is going on in a picture and build up a story around it. An adult could act as scribe or help them to key in their story and add the picture from the CD-ROM. **Vocabulary:** *birthday, breakfast, face paint, garden, Halloween, ill, lunch, lunchbox, make-up, medicine, money, Mothers' Day, piggybank, plant, present, pumpkin, saving, television, watering can.*		66
Zoo plan: 1 and 2		**Zoo plan: 1 and 2** encourage the children to use talk to clarify their thinking, and to interact with others, take turns in conversation and negotiate plans as they work together to decide which animals could live in the zoo enclosure in the picture. Model the kind of statements that they could make in this discussion: for example, *I think... because...* The activity could be linked with Science (Knowledge and understanding of the world) as the children use what they know (and perhaps find out more) about animals' needs for food and shelter and the conditions they need (for example, water) to help them to choose. They will also need to consider which animals might eat one another and therefore should not be kept together. It could also be used to show them how to use information books. **Vocabulary:** *animal, feed, pen, pond, zoo.*		67–68

		EYFS Scale Point 5	

1. Speaking
4. Drama
8. Engaging and responding to texts

Use language to imagine and recreate roles and experiences

Title		Page
Toy story		69
Postman's knock		70
The plaster cast		71
At the dentist's		
Mr Dingle's day		72
The tower		73
Finger puppets		
Billy goat mask		74
Troll mask		75
The little red hen		76–77
		78

Toy story gives the children an opportunity to imagine and recreate roles and experiences. Speaking as if they were a toy will help them to talk to an audience as this helps to lessen their feelings of exposure and provides a sense of security. You could also let the children bring in their own teddy bear or other toy character and tell a story about what it has been doing. **Vocabulary:** *once upon a time, one day, pretend, story.*

Postman's knock focuses on using talk to imagine and recreate experiences. Ask the children what happens when the post comes to their house, especially if there is something that cannot be pushed through the letterbox. What might they say to the postman (or woman)? What might he or she say? This could be linked with work in Citizenship (Taking part – developing skills of communication and participation) and in Geography (Knowledge and understanding of the world). You could focus on polite greetings and farewells: *hello, good morning, good afternoon, goodbye, see you tomorrow.* **Vocabulary:** *letter, letterbox, mail, parcel, post, postman.*

The plaster cast provides a scenario to encourage the children to use talk to imagine and recreate experiences. Some children might be able to talk about their own injuries or those of friends or members of their families. You could link this with work in Citizenship (Choices), with a focus on safe choices and avoiding accidents and in Science – ourselves (Knowledge and understanding of the world). The activity could also be used in conjunction with a 'hospital' role-play area. You could introduce words such as *ache, aching, bone, break, broken, fracture, pain, painful, sling, surgeon.* Model the sort of language that children will use: for example, *She broke her arm.* **Vocabulary:** *bone, break, broken, doctor, fracture, hospital, nurse, plaster cast.*

At the dentist's provides a setting to foster the use of talk to imagine and recreate roles and experiences. After the children have talked about the picture with a friend, an adult could help them to write, or could act as scribe, to record some of the things they said. They could use this to help them to tell their group what is happening in the picture. This could be linked with work in Science – ourselves (Knowledge and understanding of the world). **Vocabulary:** *check-up, dentist, examine, filling, tooth.*

Mr Dingle's day develops skills in using talk to imagine and recreate roles and experiences and in speaking with confidence. It provides pictures to support oral storytelling to a group or to the class. The children could take turns to tell the story of a picture in order to contribute to a collaborative story. They could talk about what might happen in the last picture and then draw their own idea. During the plenary session they could tell their version of the story. You could record the story to encourage them to make it sound interesting. You could use the CD-ROM to delete the pictures to provide a blank page for the children's own story. **Vocabulary:** *bathroom, breakfast, ducks, newspaper, park, shower, squash, wake, walk, wind, woke.*

The tower focuses on using talk to imagine and recreate roles and experiences and on speaking clearly and with confidence. They could talk in pairs about the pictures and about the order in which they happened. This will require them to say what is happening so that they should be able to tell the story afterwards. When they tell the story invite them to say how the children's feelings changed in each picture, and why. Ask them: *Why is x crying? What do you think he wanted to do?* You could invite them to change the story to make it happier. **Vocabulary:** *blocks, bricks, build, cry, down, fall, knock, tower.*

Finger puppets provides the opportunity to introduce the term 'characters' to the children. Read the story of *Goldilocks and the Three Bears* to the children. Read the story of *Goldilocks and the Three Bears* with the class, then ask them to name the characters in the story. Discuss what each character says and does. For the extension activity, the children could make a puppet for the new character. During the plenary session, groups could perform the story. Invite those watching to comment on and praise the performance. **Vocabulary:** *act, bear, character, Goldilocks, puppet, story, three.*

Billy goat mask and **Troll mask** encourage the children to read the the story of *The Three Billy Goats Gruff* (available in the Ladybird series) and focus on what each character does and says. Draw out the repetitive language: for example, 'Trip-trap, trip-trap. Who's that trip-trapping across my bridge?' To cut out the eye holes in the masks, fold them into semi-circles before cutting. Make the ear loops as shown below.

Ask the children what each billy goat did and said, drawing out the differences. Help the children to decide on a different 'voice' for each goat. Ask what the troll said and let the children practise speaking in a troll voice; discuss how this is different from the goats' voices. **Vocabulary:** *act, billy goat, character, mask, story, troll.*

The little red hen focuses on the words spoken by the animals. You could write these on a large sheet of paper and talk about which ones the cat, dog, pig and hen say. Before the children act out the story, help them to make props, such as cardboard hen's feet and animals' ears cut from card and glued onto card headbands. Encourage the children to perform to the class and to reflect on their own performances or those of others. **Vocabulary:** *act, cat, dog, hen, listen, little, pig, red, say, speak, speech bubble, story, tell.*

EYFS Scale Point 5

Speaking and listening AF1 Talk in purposeful and imaginative ways to explore ideas and feelings, adapting and varying structure and vocabulary according to purpose, listeners, and content
Speaking and listening AF1 Create and sustain different roles and scenarios, adapting techniques in a range of dramatic activities to explore texts, ideas, and issues

All Reading AFs, especially:
Reading AF6 Identify and comment on writers' purposes and viewpoints and the overall effect of the text on the reader
Reading AF3 Deduce, infer or interpret information, events or ideas from texts
Reading AF7 Relate texts to their social, cultural and historical contexts and literary traditions

Characters and words Jack goes to market	**Characters and words** is about characters' catchphrases, which are good examples of repeated and patterned language that the children can join in with and memorise. Half the children could be allocated a story character and asked to go around the room saying his or her words. The other half could carry the storybooks; they have to find their characters and the characters have to find them. They could also use the masks on pages 76–77 as templates to help them to draw masks for these characters. Let them choose a character, make the mask and then say the character's words during storyreading. You could encourage this by stopping at the point when the character is about to utter his or her catchphrase. **Jack goes to market** helps the children to make up their own alternative endings to a traditional tale. To introduce the activity, read the story of *Jack and the Beanstalk* and stop at the point where Jack is offered beans in exchange for the cow. Ask why Jack's mother wanted to sell the cow. What did she want instead? (Money to buy food) Would the beans be a good swap? Why? What should Jack do? Continue the story and, at the end, ask whether the children have changed their minds about the swap, and why. The children can then write their own stories about Jack and give them new titles: for example, *Jack and the Parrot*, *Jack and the Old Car*. Encourage them to think of happy outcomes, despite unpromising swaps. The children could enact their new stories using a box of story props such as a toy parrot, a picture of a cow (or a model/toy cow) and a large, old toy car. Encourage them to use their voices for sound effects for the cow, car and parrot as well as speaking the words of Jack and the other people. If you wish, make audio recordings of their stories, then key them in (or use voice recognition software) and print them out, adding illustrations to make a book. This activity could provide a useful starting point for speaking and listening: link it to the children's experience of 'swaps'. What have they swapped? What did they swap it for? Ask them if they and the other person were happy with the swap or if afterwards they were sorry they had swapped. Discuss whether the swaps were fair and whether they think adults should make them give things back if a swap is unfair.	79 80
Story groups: 1 and 2	**Story groups: 1** and **2** encourage the children to imagine and recreate roles. The cards depict characters from *Little Red Riding Hood* (Little Red Riding Hood, her father the woodcutter, grandma and the wolf), *Jack and the Beanstalk* (Jack, his mother, the man with the beans and the giant) and *Goldilocks and the Three Bears* (Mother Bear, Father Bear, Baby Bear and Goldilocks). Remind the children of these stories before they embark on this activity. You could set up displays about each story using the storybook, objects connected with the story, pictures of the characters, audio recordings and so on. The activities provide opportunities for developing skills in speaking and listening (discussion with others and co-operation in finding the other characters) and drama, as the children enact the roles on their cards. As an extension activity you could mix up some of the characters: for example, group Little Red Riding Hood with Goldilocks, Jack and the giant, so that the children can make up and enact a new story. If possible, make a video recording of their stories to show on the computer. Display it on an interactive whiteboard with a split screen so that you can key in some of the words they say, such as, 'What big teeth you have!' or 'Someone has been climbing my beanstalk!' You could laminate the pages for re-use.	81–82

12

Linking sounds and letters

Activity name	Strand and learning objectives	Notes on the activities	Assessment Focus	Page number
Alphabet action song	**5. Word recognition: decoding (reading) and encoding (spelling)** Link sounds to letters, naming and sounding the letters of the alphabet	**Alphabet action song** uses rhyme and actions to help the children to learn the names of the 26 letters of the alphabet and the order. It also helps to introduce some of the sounds they can represent in writing. Use the CD-ROM to display the text on an interactive whiteboard. The song, or sections of it, could be sung at the beginning or end of any lesson. Encourage the children to sing it in their free time and to do the actions.	**EYFS Scale Point 4** **Reading AF1** Use a range of strategies including accurate decoding of text, to read for meaning **Writing AF8** Use correct spelling	83
Start the same		**Start the same** provides practice in discriminating the consonant phonemes /t/, /p/, /n/, /m/ and /d/ and learning the letters that represent them in writing. The focus is on the initial consonant and, since the children are not asked to read the entire words, some of them have more than one vowel and some are polysyllabic words. You could also play games in which the children look at, handle and name collections of objects beginning with the same letter and place the appropriate wooden or plastic letter beside the collection. Also make up alliterative sentences with the children: for example, *Peter picked a piece of paper, Postman Pat posted a potato, Naughty Natasha needs nine nails, Nina nodded and neighed, Mina makes a messy muddle, Mister Men mix mangoes and mud, Dinosaurs danced and dazzled, Ducks dine on Delia's doughnuts.*		84
Odd one out		**Odd one out** helps the children to link sounds to letters. It provides practice in discriminating the phonemes /g/, /o/ and /k/ and learning the letters that represent them in writing (note that **c** and **k** can both stand for the /k/ phoneme). The focus is on the initial consonant and, since the children are not asked to read the entire words, some of them have more than one vowel and some are polysyllabic words. You could also play games in which the children look at, handle and name collections of objects beginning with the same letter but which also contain an 'odd' item that begins with a different letter.		85
Missing a Missing i o in the middle	**5. Word recognition: decoding (reading) and encoding (spelling)** Hear and say sounds in words in the order in which they occur	**Missing a** and **Missing i** help the children to hear and say sounds in words in the order in which they occur, to segment and write CVC words with the medial vowel phonemes /a/ and /i/, respectively, and then to blend the phonemes to read the words. You could also provide plastic letters that have been taught and ask them to make other words and names on phoneme frames with three boxes: for example (using only the /a/ vowel phoneme), *Dan, man, map, sad, sap, sat, tan*; (using only the /i/ vowel phoneme) *dim, din, dip, pit, Tim*. Alternatively, provide phoneme frames on an interactive white-board with the letters the children can key the words. You could also use the CD-ROM to edit the page for re-use with other medial vowels and with other initial and final consonants. **o in the middle** provides practice in discriminating the medial vowel phoneme /o/. The cards can be used in various ways (see the Teachers' note at the bottom of the page). At this stage the cards are intended to be used for oral work, since they include letters that have not yet been taught: the CCVC words *frog* and *clock*.	**EYFS Scale Point 5** **Reading AF1** Use a range of strategies including accurate decoding of text, to read for meaning **Writing AF8** Use correct spelling	86–87
Missing e		**Missing e** and **Missing u** help the children to segment and write CVC words with the medial vowel phonemes /e/ and /u/, respectively, and then to blend the phonemes and read the words. You could also provide plastic letters that have been taught and ask them to make other words and names on phoneme grids with three boxes: for example (using the /e/ vowel phoneme), *deck, get, keg, Ken, Meg, men, met, neck, Ned, net, peck, peg, pen, red, Ted, Teg* (Welsh); (using the /u/ vowel phoneme) *cup, duck, dug, gum, gut, muck, mug, rug, run, rut, suck, sum, sup, tuck, tug*. You could also use the CD-ROM to edit the page for re-use with other medial vowels and with other initial and final consonants.		88
Missing u The mill on the hill Names with ss		**The mill on the hill** and **Names with ss** focus on discriminating the phonemes /l/ and /s/ and segmenting words that contain these sounds in order to spell them using the **ll** and **ss** graphemes. It is useful to point out that, in English, very few short words end in **l** or **s** (exceptions include *bus, gas, gel, nil* and the names *Gus, Hal, Lil, Mel and Val*) and that none begins with **ll** or **ss**. Other useful words and names include (**ll**) *dell, Hell, Nell, sell; bill, Bill, fill, sill, till; bull, dull, full, Hull, Hull;* (**ss**) *mass, pass; less, mess; hiss, kiss, miss; boss, loss, moss, Ross, toss; fuss.*		89–90
Letter change		**Letter change** focuses on hearing and saying sounds in words in the order in which they occur and writing one grapheme for each phoneme. This activity provides an opportunity to link early phonic work with the children's early writing of patterns, curves and joins. It is also useful to have letter tiles available for them to try out their proposed word as necessary. The children should place the letter tiles in the gaps on the sheet and only write the letters once they are happy they have made a real word. You could use the CD-ROM to adapt the pages so that different phonemes and graphemes are practised (see Letters and Sounds, pages 126-8).		91–92
Missing v		**Missing v** is about using, hearing and discriminating phonemes and learning the graphemes that represent them: here the focus is on the /v/ phoneme. You could begin, orally, with silly sentences with alliterative /v/ sounds: *Vera visits Val's velvet vegetables, Vic's vacuum cleaner is very vast.* You could read out a list of words and ask the children to indicate when they hear a /v/ sound in the middle: include *clover, even, ever, heaven, hover, liver, loaves, love, never, ourselves, seven, sleeve, themselves, wave, weaving, woven.*		93
Missing x		**Missing x** is about hearing and discriminating the /ks/ phoneme in a word, hearing and saying sounds in words in the order in which they occur and using phonic knowledge to write simple words. Other simple words the children could write include *fax, ox, six, tax, vex.* You could also use the CD-ROM to edit the page for re-use with other medial vowels and with other initial consonants.		94
Yan says yes		**Yan says yes** focuses on hearing and discriminating the **y** phoneme in a word, hearing and saying sounds in words in the order in which they occur and using phonic knowledge to write simple words. You could also read lists of words and names that include some beginning with **y** and ask the children to indicate when they hear a word beginning with **y**. You could also use the CD-ROM to edit the page for re-use with other words and names: for example, *yacht, yard, Yasmin, year, yesterday, yet, yolk, Yorkshire, you, young, your.*		95
				96

	5. Word recognition: decoding (reading) and encoding (spelling) 6. Word structure and spelling Use phonic knowledge to write simple regular words and make phonetically plausible attempts at more complex words			EYFS Scale Point 6 **Reading AF1** Use a range of strategies including accurate decoding of text, to read for meaning **Writing AF8** Use correct spelling
Word writer: 1, 2 and 3		**Word writer: 1, 2, 3** and **4** focus on hearing and saying sounds in words in the order in which they occur and writing one grapheme for each phoneme. These activities provide an opportunity to link early phonic work with the children's early writing of patterns, curves and joins. It is also useful to have letter tiles available for them to try out their proposed word as necessary. The children should place the letter tiles in the gaps on the sheet and only write the letters once they are happy they have made a real word. You could use the CD-ROM to adapt the pages so that different phonemes and graphemes are practised (see *Letters and Sounds*, pages 126–8).	97–100	
Word writer: 4				
The king sings		**The king sings** develops skills in segmenting words ending with /**ng**/. You could encourage the children to play with words in making up 'The king's song', which might begin *The king sang a song about banging on a gong, with his gang of singers and their fangs. The king sang a song about flinging things on strings, with his ring of jingling singers in their bling....*	101	
Cats and mice		**Cats and mice** helps the children to segment and write simple CVC words with the medial vowel phoneme /**ar**/, and then to blend the phonemes and read the words. They try different letters in the gaps, read the words and decide whether they are real words, before choosing the correct letter. The children will find that some letters will complete more than one word correctly. As a further extension activity, challenge them to complete the page in a way that does not use the same letter twice: *harm, park, cart, yard.* Other words they could make, if using a letter more than once, include *card, hard, hark* and *part.*	102	
Hens and eggs		**Hens and eggs** helps the children to segment and write simple CVC words with the medial vowel phonemes /**ai**/, /**igh**/, /**ee**/ and /**ow**/, and then to blend the phonemes and read the words. They try different letters in the gaps, read the words and decide whether they are real words, before choosing the correct letter group.	103	
Add and change: 1 and 2		**Add and change: 1** and **2** focus on discriminating and writing the final consonant in CVCC words and the initial consonant in CCVC words, respectively. Other CVCC words that could be read aloud for the children to make with plastic letters or write on phoneme frames include *band, bank, bend, bent, bump, camp, daft, damp, dent, dump, gift, hand, honk, hunt, jump, junk, lamp, land, left, lift, limp, link, loft, lump, mint, pink, pump, sand, sank, send, sent, soft, sunk, tank, tent, think, went, wind, wink.* Other CCVC words include *black, bleep, block, brain, brick, brim, bring, clang, clap, clash, class, click, cliff, cling, clop, cloth, crack, cram, crash, flash, flick, fling, flip, fluff, fresh, frill, slam, slap, sleep, slim, slip, slosh, smack, snap, sniff, snug, speck, spill, spit, squid, stack, stick, stuck, stem, step, stiff, still, stop, stuff, swim, swing, swish, track, train, trap, trick, trim, trip, twang, twin.*	104–105	
Teddy talk		**Teddy talk** develops skills in segmenting and spelling CVCC words using grapheme–phoneme correspondence. Other words the children could segment and spell include: *belt, felt, melt, best, chest, rest, west, boast, coast, burnt, dust, just, must, rust, film, fist, list, mist, help, yelp, mask, self, shelf, silk, sulk, task.*	106	

Reading

Activity name	Strand and learning objectives	Notes on the activities	Assessment Focus	Page number
In the hat	5. Word recognition: decoding (reading) and encoding (spelling) Explore and experiment with sounds, words and text	In the hat, In the bag, On the fence and Looking for l and Looking for l provide practice in discriminating the phonemes /f/, /h/, /b/, /l/ and /l/ and learning the letters that represent them in writing. The focus is on the initial consonant and, since the children are not asked to read the entire words, some of them are polysyllabic words. Some children could also draw extra items in the pictures, ensuring that they begin with the correct letter. You could also play games in which the children complete sentences such as In my bag I have a … ball, banana, basket, bat, bell, biscuit, bone, book; In my hat I have a … hairbrush, hairpin, handbag, handkerchief, handle, helmet, humbug; On the fence I see a … fan, fig, fork, four, fur; On the ladder I see a … ladybird, leaf, lemon, letter, lime, lock, locket, lollipop.	**EYFS Scale Point 5** **Reading AF1** Use a range of strategies including accurate decoding of text, to read for meaning **Writing AF8** Use correct spelling	107–110
In the bag				
On the fence				
Looking for l				
In the jar	5. Word recognition: decoding (reading) and encoding (spelling) Read and write one grapheme for each of the 44 phonemes	In the jar provides practice in discriminating the phoneme /j/ and learning the letter that represents it in writing. The focus is on the initial consonant and, since the children are not asked to read the entire word, some words have more than one vowel and some are polysyllabic. You could sing 'silly songs' (or 'jingles') that feature alliterative /j/ sounds with the children: for example, I'm just a jelly in the jungle, jumping over juice and juggling jagged jam jars in the jungle. I wear a jazzy jersey with my jeans, and joke with jiggling jelly beans.	**EYFS Scale Point 6** **Reading AF1** Use a range of strategies including accurate decoding of text, to read for meaning **Writing AF8** Use correct spelling	111
Wet wellies		Wet wellies is about hearing and discriminating the /w/ phoneme at the beginning of a word. You could also set the children a 'w treasure hunt' in which they have to find objects (pictures of them) that begin with w: for example, wall, wasp, water, well, window, wire. Words the children could read, or write using phoneme frames, include wag, web, well, wet, wick, wig, will, win, wit, wok, woof. Silly sentences with w: William walked up the wall, Walruses wear wet wellies, A worm wore a woollen waistcoat.		112
z or s?		z or s? is about hearing the /z/ phoneme at the beginning of a word and discriminating it from the /s/ phoneme. The children could also blend and read or segment and spell simple words and names such as Zak, zap, zip, and the two-syllable word zigzag. Alliterative sentences for the children to repeat are Zena the zany zebra zoomed, zipped and zigzagged around the zoo and Sam the silly seal sang, sailed and swam in the sunshine.		113
Sheena's ship		Sheena's ship and Chuck's chat help the children to hear and discriminate the /sh/ and /ch/ phonemes in a word. They could also blend and read or segment and spell simple words and names displayed on an interactive whiteboard, such as (sh) shack, shall, shell, shin, ship, shock, shop, shot, shut, ash, bash, cash, dash, gash, lash, mash, rash, sash, mesh, dish, fish, wish, posh, bush, mush, push, rush; (ch) chap, chat, check, chess, chick, chin, chill, chip, chop, chuck, chum, rich, such. You could play a game called 'Sheena's ship' in which the children repeat an alliterative sentence and then add to it: for example, On Sheena's ship I saw a fish; On Sheena's ship I saw a fish and a shop: On Sheena's ship I saw a fish, a shop and a shoe: On Sheena's ship I saw a fish, a shop, a shoe and a shower…. Similarly, play 'Chuck's chat': Chuck chatted about some cheese; Chuck chatted about some cheese and some chocolate; Chuck chatted about some cheese, some chocolate and a chain; Chuck chatted about some cheese, some chocolate, a chain and a chimpanzee…		114–115
Chuck's chat				
Find our foods		Find our foods focuses on the initial sounds of words. You could read some poems and rhymes featuring alliteration and emphasise the alliterative sounds (for example, Simple Simon and Lucy Locket). Once the children have completed the activity, encourage them to make up sentences about one another and foods by asking questions: for example, Who eats potatoes? The children answer with an alliterative sentence: Peter eats potatoes. Other examples include Carla likes carrots, Dina likes dates, Fawzia likes fish, Gary likes grapes, Hasan likes hummus. This could also be reinforced with picture/card matching, or with children choosing pictures of foods that share the initial sound of their name.		116
Slippery slimy		Slippery slimy helps the children to appreciate the quality of sounds. You could make a 'slippery slimy' material for the children to handle and talk about: mix cornflour with water until it has a thick, slippery consistency or make jelly from jelly crystals and let them explore its texture. Commercially produced 'slimy' materials are also available. Encourage the children to describe the feel and sound of the 'slime'. The words crispy crunchy can also be explored by comparing foods and materials and saying if they are 'crispy crunchy'. You could investigate celery, radishes, crisps, biscuits, thin pieces of wood that snap, dry leaves and tissue paper, comparing them with jelly, mud, sponge, fur and so on.		117
Flip, flap		Flip, flap provides an opportunity to play with sounds. You could set up a 'flip, flap' table with a collection of objects that make a 'flip, flap' sound or movement: sheets of thin card stapled together at one end, pieces of cloth, a flag, a shoe with a loose sole. When playing the game, the children could draw or write the names of the things they land on that go 'flip, flap' and use these ideas to help them make up a poem or rhyme: for example, Flip-flap, washing, Flapping on the line, Flip-flap, washing, Flapping all the time, or Flip-flap, tail, Wagging back and forth, Flip-flap, tail, Wagging south and north. You could hum or 'dum' the rhythm and encourage the children to fill in the gaps: for example, Flip-flap flag, dum-de-dum-de-dum, Flip-dum, dum, Dum-de-dum-de-dum. (Supply as few or as many words as are needed to help the children.) The children can also investigate things that go 'thump, bump' or 'scratch, scrape': heavy boots, a fist on a table, a giant, a mouse, a comb on gravel and so on. You could make large game boards for these (even floor-mat sized). Link this with knowledge and understanding of the world (Science: materials).		118
In the ring		In the ring provide practice in discriminating the phonemes /r/, /h/, /b/, /l/ and /l/ and learning the letters that represent them in writing. The focus is on the initial consonant and, since the children are not asked to read the entire words, some of them have more than one vowel and some are polysyllabic words. Some children could also draw extra items in the pictures, ensuring that they begin with the correct letter. You could also play games in which the children complete sentences such as In my bag I have a … ball, banana, basket, bat, bell, biscuit, bone, book; In my hat I have a … hairbrush, hairpin, handbag, handkerchief, handle, helmet, humbug; On the fence I see a … fan, fig, fork, four, fur; On the ladder I see a … ladybird, leaf, lemon, letter, lime, lock, locket, lollipop.		119

Activity	Objective	Description	EYFS / Assessment Focus	Page
Real words, wacky words: 1	**5. Word recognition: decoding (reading) and encoding (spelling)** Read simple words by sounding out and blending the phonemes all through the word from left to right	**Real words, wacky words: 1** develops skills in reading simple words by sounding out and blending the phonemes all through the word from left to right and then deciding whether the word makes sense. You could use the CD-ROM to adapt this page so that different CVC words are presented, to practise reading other phonemes the children have learned (see *Letters and Sounds*, page 126).	**EYFS Scale Point 6** **Reading AF1** Use a range of strategies including accurate decoding of text, to read for meaning **Writing AF8** Use correct spelling	120
Real words, wacky words: 2		**Real words, wacky words: 2** develops skills in reading simple words by sounding out and blending the phonemes all through the word from left to right and then deciding whether the words make sense. You could use the CD-ROM to adapt this page so that different words are presented, to practise reading other phonemes the children have learned (see *Letters and Sounds*, page 127).		121
Real words, wacky words: 3		**Real words, wacky words: 3** develops skills in reading two-syllable words, especially those ending with the **/er/** phoneme, by sounding out and blending the phonemes all through the word from left to right and then deciding whether the words make sense. You could use the CD-ROM to adapt this page so that different words are presented, to practise reading other phonemes the children have learned (see *Letters and Sounds*, page 128).		122
Match-up: 1 and 2		**Match-up: 1** and **2** provide practice in blending and reading simple words containing, respectively, the phonemes **/or/** and **/ur/**/**oi/** and **/ear/**. Other useful two-syllable **/ur/** and **/ear/** words include *further, turnip; gearbox*.		123–124
Match-up: 3		**Match-up: 3** provides practice in blending and reading two-syllable words containing the **/er/** phoneme as in *boxer*. Other useful two-syllable **/er/** words include *banger, boiler, further, joiner, longer, murder, offer, packer, shorter, singer, suffer, surfer*. The children could also add **-er** to one-syllable words: for example, *burn → burner, curl → curler, farm → farmer, fight → fighter, mill → miller, peel → peeler*.		125
Sound change: 1 and 2		**Sound change: 1** and **2** is about blending and reading CVC words with the medial vowel phonemes **/ee/, /ai/, /oo/, /igh/, /oa/, /or/** and **/ur/**. The children begin to develop an understanding that spelling is the reverse of blending phonemes into words for reading, through changing the medial vowel. You could also play games in which the children take turns to change part of a word in order to make a new one and continue changing until they get back to the original word: for example, *sight → soot → sort → fort → feet → fight → sight*.		126–127
Sound machines		**Sound machines** focuses on blending and reading words that contain the vowel phonemes **/air/ /ear/ /oi/** and **/ure/**. You could also use the CD-ROM to alter the letters in the phoneme grids or the vowel phonemes in the sound machines.		128
Two letters, one sound: 1	**5. Word recognition: decoding (reading) and encoding (spelling)** Recognise common digraphs	**Two letters – one sound: 1** helps the children to recognise the common digraph **ck**, to say and write CVC words ending in **-ck**, and then blend the phonemes to read the words. Other useful words and names that could be used on adapted versions of the page include *buck, dock, kick, muck, neck, nick, pick, rack, Rick, rock, sock, suck, tack, tuck*. You could also introduce a few two-syllable words: for example, *backpack, cockpit, pocket, rucksack*.	**EYFS Scale Point 8** **Reading AF1** Use a range of strategies including accurate decoding of text, to read for meaning **Writing AF8** Use correct spelling	129
Two letters, one sound: 2		**Two letters – one sound: 2** helps the children to hear and discriminate the **/s/** and **/z/** phonemes at the ends of words and to spell words accurately using grapheme–phoneme correspondence. It is useful to point out that few English words end in **z** – **zz** is more common.		130
Two letters, one sound: 3		**Two letters – one sound: 3** provides practice in recognising the common digraph **th** in words and using grapheme–phoneme correspondence to help the children to spell words containing the phoneme **/th/**: this includes **/th/** as in *the* and *with* and **/th/** as in *thin* and *both*. Other words and names they could blend and read or segment and spell, perhaps displayed on an interactive whiteboard, include *then, this, thud, both, Beth, moth, path*.		131
Partners: 1 and 2		**Partners: 1** and **2** provide practice in blending and reading simple words containing, respectively, the digraphs or trigraphs **ai, ee, ar, ch, sh, th** and **ck**, and **igh, oa, oo** (as in *soon*), **or, ow, qu** and **oi**. Use these for matching games, as outlined in the Teachers' notes on the pages, or give the children the pictures, help them to sound-talk the words and ask them to write the words, key them in or use plastic letters to spell them. The children could also group most of the pictures, with the words, according to the main sound they hear when they say them: **/oa/, /ai/, /ee/, /ar/, /oo/, /ow/**. You could read out other words and ask the children to point to a picture (with its caption word) that has the same sound. Useful words and names for this include *aid, paid, raid, aid, fail, hail, mail, sail, tail, wail, gain, main, pain, rain: deed, feed, need, seed, seek, seem, deep, weep, feet, sheet; march, hard, lard, ark, bark, dark, hark, lark, park, shark, Carl, Karl, charm, harm, barn, marsh, cart, chart, dart, part; fight, might, right; foal, goal, foam, loaf, poach, road, soak, toad: boom, room, food, mood, hoof, roof, pool, tool, noon, soon, hoop, loop, root, shoot; porch, cork, fork, pork, born, corn, thorn, torn, fort, port, short, sort, north; sow* (meaning pig), *down, gown, town, howl, jowl; quack, quail, quick, quid, quit; oil, boil, coil, foil, soil, coin, join*. Useful two-syllable words: *again, raining, indeed, soaking, morning, towel, joining*.		132–133
Ready for action: words	**5. Word recognition: decoding (reading) and encoding (spelling)** Read a range of familiar and common words and simple sentences independently	**Ready for action: words, Ready for action: pictures** and **Question cards** develop skills in reading fluently and automatically by using phonic knowledge of grapheme–phoneme correspondence and blending as the prime approach for decoding unfamiliar words. The cards can be used in various ways (see the Teachers' notes on the pages). An additional activity could be for one child or group of children to mime an action from an action picture word card while a partner or another group seek out the matching action word card. The children could also build longer sentences based on the	**EYFS Scale Point 6** **Reading AF1** Use a range of strategies including accurate decoding of text, to read for meaning **Writing AF8** Use correct spelling	134 135
Ready for action: pictures				
Question cards	**5. Word recognition: decoding (reading) and encoding (spelling)** Read texts compatible with their phonic knowledge and skills	**Ready for action** cards: for example, by starting with *I can ...* or *We can ...*	**EYFS Scale Point 9** **Reading AF1** Use a range of strategies including accurate decoding of text, to read for meaning **Writing AF8** Use correct spelling	136

Activity	Objectives	Description	Assessment	Page
Titles Page match Place to place	**7. Understanding and responding to texts** Know that print carries meaning and, in English, is read from left to right and top to bottom	**Titles** introduces the term *title* and focuses on the main characters named in the titles. Discuss who the 'most important' character is in each story and make the link with the title – are titles always the name of the main character only? – for example, *Goldilocks and the Three Bears*. You could also ask the children how the story begins, what the character does, what happens to him/her/it and how the story ends. **Page match** is about the events that take place in stories. The children could begin by looking at the covers of books, identifying the titles and then talking about the characters. Ask them what the characters did and what happened to them. During plenary sessions the children could hold up a book they have read, point out and read the title, say who the characters are and then say, briefly, what happened to them and what they did. Encourage the others to listen and then to ask questions about why characters did particular actions. The children could answer questions 'in role' as story characters after enacting these roles in small groups. **Place to place** focuses on the direction of text from left to right. Encourage the children to walk their fingers along the footsteps as they read each word, emphasising where the sentence starts and the direction in which they read it. You could also chalk sentences on giant footprints in the playground (from left to right) and help the children to read them as they follow the trail.	**EYFS Scale Point 4** **Reading AF2** Understand, describe, select or retrieve information, events or ideas from texts and use quotation and reference to text **Reading AF3** Deduce, infer or interpret information, events or ideas from texts **Reading AF1** Use a range of strategies including accurate decoding of text, to read for meaning **Reading AF4** Identify and comment on the structure and organization of texts, including grammatical and presentational features at text level **Reading AF5** Explain and comment on writers' uses of language, including grammatical and literary features at word and sentence level	137 138 139
Name rhymes Same starters Acker Backer Dip, dip, dip	**1. Speaking** **2. Listening and responding** **7. Understanding and responding to texts** Extend their vocabulary, exploring the meanings and sounds of new words	**Name rhymes** develops the children's appreciation of rhyme. They could first say their own names and see if they can think of any words that rhyme with them (or with the last syllable of longer names). They could also make up rhyming lines using the names on the page (and other names): for example, *Mary Ann waved her fan*, *Little Lee went to sea*, *My friend Ben had a hen*, *Jo, Jo stuck out her toe*, *Ed, Ed, where's your head?*, *My friend Grace has a lovely face*. **Same starters** focuses on the initial sounds of words and can be linked with work in phonics. The children could make up similar examples about themselves and others in the class: for example, *Bella bounces*, *Clare claps*, *Charlie chooses*, *Deepak dives*, *Peter paints*. **Acker Backer** encourages the children to enjoy a clapping rhyme which they say and play with a partner, making one clap or slap for each word. Most children find this catchy rhyme fun to say or sing at playtime and spontaneously make up their own actions. They could also make up or suggest other 'Acker' words: for example, 'Acker Macker' or 'Acker Slacker'. The entire class could recite the rhyme, with the actions, in a large space such as a playground or hall. **Health and safety**: Clapping actions, in which the children touch a partner, should involve the touching of hands only; in the slapping actions the children should slap only themselves: for example, slap their own thighs or bottom. **Dip, dip, dip** develops the children's understanding of rhythm as they join in by tapping a finger on a sailor as each word is spoken. Some children will be familiar with 'dips' used as a fair way of selecting someone to do something or for eliminating children from a group in order to select a winner. One child points to each member of the group in turn as each word of the 'dip' is recited. The child he or she stops on is 'out'; this continues until only one remains.	**EYFS Scale Point 9** **Speaking and listening AF1** Talk in purposeful and imaginative ways to explore ideas and feelings, adapting and varying structure and vocabulary according to purpose, listeners, and content **Speaking and listening AF2** Listen and respond to others, including in pairs and groups, shaping meanings through suggestions, comments, and questions **Speaking and listening AF4** Understand the range and uses of spoken language, commenting on meaning and impact and draw on this when talking to others **Reading AF2** Understand, describe, select or retrieve information, events or ideas from texts and use quotation and reference to text **Reading AF3** Deduce, infer or interpret information, events or ideas from texts **Reading AF1** Use a range of strategies including accurate decoding of text, to read for meaning **Reading AF4** Identify and comment on the structure and organization of texts, including grammatical and presentational features at text level **Reading AF5** Explain and comment on writers' uses of language, including grammatical and literary features at word and sentence level	140 141 142 143

Activity	Pages	Objectives	AFs
Character match: 1 and 2	144–145	**7. Understanding and responding to texts** **8. Engaging and responding to texts** Show an understanding of the elements of stories, such as main character, sequence of events, and openings, and how information can be found in non-fiction texts to answer questions about where, who, why and how	**EYFS Scale Point 5** **Reading AF2** Understand, describe, select or retrieve information, events or ideas from texts and use quotation and reference to text **Reading AF3** Deduce, infer or interpret information, events or ideas from texts **Reading AF1** Use a range of strategies including accurate decoding of text, to read for meaning **Reading AF4** Identify and comment on the structure and organization of texts, including grammatical and presentational features at text level **Reading AF5** Explain and comment on writers' uses of language, including grammatical and literary features at word and sentence level
Story things match	146		
Lost characters	147		
The wrong order			
Story route cards			
Information books	148	**5. Word recognition: decoding (reading) and encoding (spelling)** Read a range of familiar and common words and simple sentences independently	All Reading AFs, especially: **Reading AF6** Identify and comment on writers' purposes and viewpoints and the overall effect of the text on the reader **Reading AF3** Deduce, infer or interpret information, events or ideas from texts **Reading AF7** Relate texts to their social, cultural and historical contexts and literary traditions
Baby animals	149		
Animal families	150		
Animal homes			
Plants	151–154		**EYFS Scale Point 6** **Reading AF1** Use a range of strategies including accurate decoding of text, to read for meaning **Writing AF8** Use correct spelling
How to make chocolate crispies			
Now and then	155		
Party time	156		
	157		

Character match: 1 and 2 are about the characters in popular traditional tales. Characters from stories the children do not know can be removed when the cards are cut out. When reading stories with the children, ask them whom the stories are about and introduce the term 'character', which can mean a person or an animal. You could begin by giving each child a different character card and asking them who they are and what happened in their stories. These cards can be used in several ways: spread out the cards, face up, and ask the children to make pairs of characters from the same story; or, as a more challenging activity, introduce an element of competition by spreading out the cards face down and asking the children to take turns to turn over two cards (they keep the pairs and the one with the most pairs when all have been picked up is the winner). Alternatively, to develop speaking and listening skills, you could give a card to each child and ask them to find their partner from the same story. They could enact the story with their partner. The children could add their own cards, using pairs of characters from other stories they know.

Story things match focuses on important objects in stories. After reading a story with the children, ask them about some of the things in the story: for example, the straw, the sticks and the bricks in *The Three Little Pigs*; the porridge, the chairs and the beds in *Goldilocks*. As for the previous activity, you could encourage the development of speaking and listening skills by giving half the group a character card (use just one character from each story) and the other half an object card and asking them to find their partners. To make the activity more demanding, use both sets of character cards and ask the children to form groups of three: two characters and the object from the story. The cards could also be used as 'dressing-up' clothes. You could make a display about a different story, which could be changed each week and which includes important objects and materials as well as 'dressing-up' clothes. The children could also collect or make objects for the display. Once the children know several stories, hold up an object during plenary sessions and ask the children which story it is from or which story character might need it. Also ask how the object was used in the story or what it was for.

Lost characters consolidates the children's learning about characters as they match the characters to the stories. This activity is suitable for use with a group of children or introduced as a group activity. You will probably need to talk to the children about each book cover and help them to read the title and then to identify the characters who belong to the story. Ask them who else is in that story and help them to find one of those characters (or group of them) on another book cover. The children could also draw pictures of events from other stories based on these pictures, in which the new character changes the story. Some children might be able to make up new stories based on these pictures, in which the new character changes the story. You could also make story maps that can be laid out on the floor and help the children to draw, colour and cut out characters from stories they know. The children can then place the characters on the story maps, move them around and develop dialogue and action with other characters. This could include characters who 'get lost' from their own stories and end up in the wrong ones. The children could help them to find their way back.

The wrong order is about the sequence of events in a story. This page focuses on *The Gingerbread Man*. Ask the children about the title and characters of the story and then what happened at the beginning. You could read together the opening words: for example, *Once upon a time.... One day.... There was once...* What did the Gingerbread Man do? What did the other characters do? Did the Gingerbread Man get away? Ask the children what happened at the end of the story and whether this was a happy ending. Before they glue the pages from the activity onto a sheet, ask the children to tell the story using the pictures. Do they look right? If not, they should change the order.

Story route cards is about the main events of a story and their sequence. You could begin by drawing attention to the opening words of a story: ask the children to begin telling the story with an opening such as *Once upon a time.... One day...* or *There was once...* The pictures help them to tell the main events of the story in the correct sequence. Model time connectives such as *then, next, after that* and *the next day* in retellings. The endings of the stories have been omitted so that the children can draw pictures to help them to finish the story.

Information books focuses on how to use non-fiction books to find information and how to choose the most useful book to find information on a particular topic. The children could also choose non-fiction books about particular subjects from the class or school library. Invite volunteers to talk to the class about a non-fiction book they have read, saying what it was about and what they found out from it. It is useful to draw out how these books are different from storybooks.

Baby animals, **Animal families**, **Animal homes** and **Plants** are about finding information from non-fiction books about baby animals and plants. The children can find information on these pages which they then use to help them to complete labels and sentences. During the plenary session point out that they used non-fiction pages to find out what they needed to know. These activities could be linked with work in Knowledge and understanding of the world (Science) lessons. Also show the children non-fiction books about other topics linked to Knowledge and understanding of the world (Science) lessons. Model how to choose and use the books by 'thinking aloud'.

How to make chocolate crispies is about using a non-fiction text to find out how to do something. The children learn that the text in instructions has to be presented in the correct order so that it makes sense to the reader. As a further extension, they could number the pictures when they have them in the correct order. This could be linked to Knowledge and understanding of the world (science) lessons: the children could use the words 'liquid' and 'solid' when working with an adult to melt chocolate.

Now and then develops the children's skills in using information books to find the answers to questions. They are required to use books which will help them to find out about equipment in homes in the past. It is useful to point out page headings and help the children to use them to predict what the page will be about. Point out that headings help readers to find the information they want. This can be linked with work in Knowledge and understanding of the world (history). Following a visit to a museum or other similar site, the children could help to set up a class 'home in the past' area containing items which might have been used in their great-great-grandparents' homes. This will provide a setting for role-play and speaking and listening.

Party time focuses on a familiar non-fiction text type: a party invitation. The children learn what a party invitation is for. Ask them what they would need to know if they were invited to a party. Focus on the questions it answers: *When?* and *Where?*

Resources	7. Understanding and responding to texts		EYFS Scale Point 7	Pages
The Three Little Pigs puppets Goldilocks puppets Little Red Hen mask Cat mask Rat mask Pig mask The Little Red Hen	Retell narratives in the correct sequence, drawing on the language patterns of stories	**The Three Little Pigs puppets** and **Goldilocks puppets** provide puppets to help the children to retell these well known stories. They could first identify the characters and say what they did and what happened to them. Discuss what the Three Little Pigs puppets are carrying, and why. Draw out that the first Little Pig made a house from straw, the second made a house from sticks and the third made a house from bricks. Ask them what the Wolf did and which house was the best. The children could compare the Three Bears: ask them which is Father Bear, which is Mother Bear and which is Baby Bear, and how they can tell. Remind them about what Goldilocks did – the order in which she tried out the chairs, tasted the porridge and lay on the beds. Also ask them about some of the things she said (too big, too small, too hot, too cold, too soft, too hard, just right). The children could retell the stories using all four finger puppets (two on each hand) but, if they find this difficult, they could work with a partner or even in a group of four in which they enact the stories. Encourage them to show how the characters feel. **Little Red Hen mask, Cat mask, Rat mask, Pig mask** and **The Little Red Hen** help the children to enact the roles of characters in *The Little Red Hen*: the Little Red Hen, the Cat, the Rat and the Pig. The words of the characters are not difficult to learn because they are repetitive: the Little Red Hen asks, 'Who will help me to...?' and the other characters reply, 'Not I,' and she replies, 'Then I will ... it myself.' The Little Red Hen then goes off to carry out the tasks of planting and watering the wheat, cutting it, taking it to the miller and taking the flour to the baker to be baked into a loaf of bread. That is, until she asks who will help her to eat the bread, whereupon the Cat, the Rat and the Pig all answer, 'I will' – 'No, you will not!' says the Little Red Hen, and eats it herself. The story contains good examples of repeated and patterned language which the children can join in and memorise. This story could be linked with discussions in Citizenship lessons about friendship and helping people. You could carry out a hot-seating activity with a child wearing a character mask and being questioned by the rest of the class about what they did, their reasons and feelings. The outlines of these masks could be used as size and shape guides and adapted to make masks of other story characters.	**Reading AF2** Understand, describe, select or retrieve information, events or ideas from texts and use quotation and reference to text **Reading AF3** Deduce, infer or interpret information, events or ideas from texts **Reading AF1** Use a range of strategies including accurate decoding of text, to read for meaning **Reading AF4** Identify and comment on the structure and organization of texts, including grammatical and presentational features at text level **Reading AF5** Explain and comment on writers' uses of language, including grammatical and literary features at word and sentence level	158–159 160–164

Writing

Activity name	Strand and learning objectives	Notes on the activities	Assessment Focus	Page number
Picture story That's wrong!	**5. Word recognition: decoding (reading) and encoding (spelling)** **6. Word structure and spelling** Use phonic knowledge to write simple regular words and make phonetically plausible attempts at more complex words	**Picture story** and **That's wrong!** develop an understanding that segmenting words into their constituent phonemes for spelling is the reverse of blending phonemes into words for reading. The children learn to spell words accurately by combining the use of grapheme–phoneme correspondence knowledge as the prime approach. **Picture story** can be linked with work on creating and shaping texts, to encourage the children to tell stories by cutting out and gluing pictures and then writing sentences about them, or keying in sentences about pictures displayed on the computer screen or interactive whiteboard.	**EYFS Scale Point 7** **Reading AF1** Use a range of strategies including accurate decoding of text, to read for meaning **Writing AF8** Use correct spelling	165 166

	Page	
9. Creating and shaping texts **10. Text structure and organisation** Attempt writing for various purposes, using features of different forms such as lists, stories and instructions		**EYFS Scale Point 6** **All Writing AFs, especially:** **Writing AF1** Write imaginative, interesting and thoughtful texts **Writing AF2** Produce texts which are appropriate to task, reader and purpose **Writing AF7** Select appropriate and effective vocabulary **Writing AF3** Organise and present whole texts effectively, sequencing and structuring information, ideas and events **Writing AF4** Construct paragraphs and use cohesion within and between paragraphs
The party	167	**The party** draws on a familiar experience: looking forward to an event. It was inspired by the story *Is It Time?* (Marilyn Janovitz, North-South) and could also be used in personal, social and emotional development (having a developing awareness of their own needs, views and feelings) and in problem-solving, reasoning and numeracy (telling the time). Ask the children about events they look forward to (or have looked forward to in the past). Discuss what it was like waiting for the event. Did they ask their parents/carers how long there was to go? Provide clock faces for the children to set at different times and encourage them to draw hands on the clock in the third picture. Ask how the story might end. What will happen at the party? In pairs, the children could enact a new story in which they are looking forward to a different event: one child asks 'Is it time for …?' and the other thinks up the responses, then they swap roles.
Map: 1 and 2	168–169	**Map: 1 and 2** develops the children's understanding of the purpose of words on maps: here they write names on a map to show who lives in each house. Link this with knowledge and understanding of the world (Geography) and focus on how words help people to understand maps. There are opportunities to link this with work in problem-solving, reasoning and numeracy (you could change the house numbers). They could add to the map: for example a park, a field, a wood, shops. These additional features could be used in recounts about the map. For the extension activity, the children should draw a simple road with several houses and write any of their friends' names next to the houses. Ask them to imagine characters going to visit a friend whose house is on the map. What might they see or hear on the way? What might they do?
The take-away	170	**The take-away** introduces lists as a context for writing. The children are asked to write a list to help 'Dad' remember what to buy at the take-away. You could enact the scene as 'Dad' with volunteers in the roles of Mum, Dan, Alex and Poppy: for example, 'What would you like, Dan?' 'Mushroom pizza, please.' This role-play could be used to foster personal, social and emotional development and skills in speaking and listening: it helps the children to understand how to take turns in a conversation and encourages good manners. You could develop this by setting up a class 'take-away' role-play corner, complete with menus, notepads and pretend food and encourage the children to say *please* and *thank you* as they ask for and receive things.
Wag goes shopping	171	**Wag goes shopping** encourages the children to write a list to help Wag the dog remember what to buy at the shops. A useful starting point is the story *Don't Forget the Bacon!* (Pat Hutchins, Red Fox), in which a little boy tries to remember everything he has been asked to fetch from the shops but gets it wrong. You could link this with personal, social and emotional development/citizenship (Animals and us): the children could list the things they need for a pet. Their lists could be part drawn and part written.
Misa's sleepover	172	**Misa's sleepover** involves writing a list to help a little girl remember to pack everything she needs for a sleepover. A useful starting point is the story *Spot Stays Overnight* (Eric Hill, Warne), in which Spot the dog goes to stay with his friend who lives next door, and packs numerous things he does not need but forgets one important item (his teddy bear). Link this with personal, social and emotional development (beginning to take responsibility for their own belongings). You could provide bags and a selection of items for the children to pack for a sleepover (toothbrushes, toothpaste, pyjamas, slippers, a change of clothes, teddy bears and so on) and long sheets of paper on which they can make lists. There are also opportunities for speaking and listening: the children could discuss in groups what they would take for a sleepover or for a seaside holiday.
At the zoo: 1 and 2	173–174	**At the zoo: 1** and **2** are about writing to give information. The children write the names of zoo animals on signs to show where they are kept. It is useful if the children first read some lift-the-flap books (both fiction and non-fiction). Also they should have opportunities to read information signs at school and in the local area: point out signs, read them together and explain what they are for. The children could find out more about the zoo animals from information books, videos or CD-ROMs so that when they lift a flap they can tell their group more about the animal pictured. They could also give clues about the animal and invite guesses from the rest of the group before lifting the flap. As an extension activity, encourage them to set up their own 'zoo corner' with pictures or model animals and signs saying what they are. High-attaining children could add warning signs, such as *Do not feed, Do not touch* or *This animal bites.*
Doors	175	**Doors** develops the children's understanding of the purpose of signs: here they write signs to tell people how to open different kinds of doors. Demonstrate the door-opening actions and ask the children to enact them to ensure that they understood them. You could show photographs of doors which have **push** and **pull** signs, and signs about the purpose of the room or building, what is in it and who may enter. This could be linked with work in knowledge and understanding of the world (Science) on pushes, pulls and other movements.
My week: 1 and 2	176–177	**My week: 1** and **2** investigate diaries as a means of recording what has happened each day. To model the activity and provide extra support, you could complete the diary on an interactive whiteboard with the whole class, focusing on the class timetable and school events. This is an opportunity to consolidate the children's knowledge of the names of the days of the week, how to spell them, and their sequence. You could read stories featuring the days of the week: for example, *The Very Hungry Caterpillar* (Eric Carle, Puffin) or *Mr Wolf's Week* (Colin Hawkins, Mammoth). After reading the story, ask the children who it was about, where the story happened, what the character did, how and why. You could also read non-fiction recounts with them (including one another's 'My week' diaries) and ask the same questions. For a more challenging activity, cut the pages into strips, mix up the days of the week and ask the children to glue them in the correct order on a large sheet of paper before they write their diary. Also let them match the names of the days in their diary to headings on a calendar.
Cinderella's shopping list	178	**Cinderella's shopping list** uses a familiar story to develop children's understanding of an everyday use of text. They should first have read or listened to the story of *Cinderella* and focused on the part where the fairy godmother sends Cinderella to find a series of items for use in her magic spells. (A pumpkin for the coach, mice for the horses, lizards for the coachmen, rats for the footmen.)
My day	179	**My day** provides an opportunity for the children to develop an understanding of an everyday use of text. This could be used to support the setting of targets during a morning or afternoon. The children could read their list to a partner, who could help them to check each item and tick it when they complete it. (You could add 'tick boxes' for this.)
Teddy bears' picnic	180	**Teddy bears' picnic** encourages the children to think about planning and to use their developing writing skills to help them in this, and provides practice in using word-banks. It could be used to support work on healthy eating in personal and social development and citizenship. The children could also write menus for school meals or for a class café, which could also be linked with work in mathematics.

Little Red Riding Hood's basket	181	**Little Red Riding Hood's basket** requires the children to read labels (supported by pictures) in order to find out information. They use labels to find out about the contents of Little Red Riding Hood's basket. In the extension activity they write their own lists. This could be linked with work in mathematics – they could write shopping lists and include the prices of the items. They could also write shopping lists for making a picnic (link this with page 177) or they could plan shopping lists for other story characters.
This way	182	**This way** develops an understanding of how signs can be used for giving information. It could be used to support work in knowledge and understanding of the world (Geography). The children could make a collage of the local area and make signs with which to indicate the locations of features. They could also make signs for the classroom or school to help visitors to find their way around.
Teddy's party	183	**Teddy's party** focuses on the use of a sentence which communicates information in a familiar context. The children could bring in party invitations they have received (or you could bring in some ready-prepared invitations for them to read). Help them to read the information on the invitations and ask them whose party they are for, on what day or date, at what time and where. Point out how the sentence is set out in order to make this information clear (the sentence is not written all on one line).
Dear Humpty Dumpty	184	**Dear Humpty Dumpty** provides an opportunity to write sentences for a purpose and to use a word-bank to support the children's writing. This could be linked with work in Citizenship and speaking and listening, in which the children could discuss safe and unsafe places to play. Their message could be to tell Humpty Dumpty how to stay safe. Read their letters with them and focus on making sense of their sentences.

Activity	11. Sentence structure and punctuation Write their own names and other things such as labels and captions and begin to form simple sentences sometimes using punctuation	Description	EYFS Scale Point 8 **Writing AF5** Vary sentences for clarity, purpose and effect **Writing AF6** Write with technical accuracy of syntax and punctuation in phrases, clauses and sentences	Page
Crazy clockroom		**Crazy clockroom** provides practice in reading names in meaningful contexts. It is useful if the children first have practice in finding one another's names around the classroom: for example, on cloakroom hooks and lunchboxes and on name cards used for activities such as registration.		185
My book		**My book** is about writing the children's names in a sentence. They practise writing their own names and those of others in a meaningful context. The children could write their names on ready-made bookplates or they could design their own. These could be scanned and duplicated for them to label some of their books.		186
Pets' corner		**Pets' corner** develops an understanding of how labels can be used for giving information and provides practice in using word-banks. It could be used to support work on animals in knowledge and understanding of the world (Science). The children could collect and label pictures of pets (their own pets, where possible) for a pets' display or models of pets for a three-dimensional model of a 'pets' corner'.		187
All wrong!		**All wrong!** develops skills in reading and understanding text in the environment and how signs can be used for giving information, and provides practice in using word-banks. Encourage the children to notice signs which help them to find their way around buildings or to know how to use places: for example, 'entrance', 'exit', 'in', 'out', 'open', 'closed', 'ladies', 'gents', 'private'.		188
Names		**Names** draws attention to the use of initial capital letters for names. The children could first find words which begin with the same letters as their names and compare the initial letters when written. Draw out that their names begin with capital letters.		189
Name that dog		**Name that dog** is about using capital letters to begin names – including the names given to animals. The children could first find out at home how to write the names of their pets or those of their friends, relations or neighbours. After completing this page they could draw feeding bowls for other dogs or cats they know and add their names.		190
Capital I		**Capital I** focuses on the personal pronoun 'I' and the use of a capital for writing it. The children could first be encouraged to say something about themselves. Draw out their use of 'I' and ask them who 'I' means. Ask them if it means the same if you say it or if someone else says it.		191
I see		**I see** focuses on the use of the personal pronoun 'I' instead of a person's name when the person is talking about himself or herself. It also reinforces the use of a capital I for writing it. The children could use a chalk board or word processor to write sentences beginning with their name and then rub out or delete their name and replace it with 'I'.		192
Starting off		**Starting off** and **Start with a capital** focus on the use of a capital letter to start a sentence. The children could also look for capital letters in books they read individually or during shared or guided reading sessions. It is also useful to provide upper- and lower-case wooden or plastic letters with which they can make up words and sentences.		193–194
Start with a capital				
A full stop		**A full stop** and **Stop it!** are about the use of a full stop to end a sentence. The children could first practise making full stops on chalk boards and on large sheets of paper in different media. They could look for the full stop on a keyboard and on the punctuation screen of a mobile phone.		195–196
Stop it!				
Full stop finder: 1 and 2		**Full stop finder: 1** and **2** develop the children's understanding that a sentence is not the same as a line of text and that a full stop ends a sentence and not a line of text. They could also find the full stops at the end of sentences in books they read, particularly those in which sentences extend over more than one line.		197–198
What did they do?		**What did they do?** focuses on verbs, although this term is not yet introduced to the children. It emphasises that a sentence says what happens or exists. This understanding can be reinforced when the children tell or write stories. An adult acting as scribe could ask the children questions about what they did and write the answers, omitting the verb, asking the children to read the sentence to check that it is correct. The children can then identify the missing word.		199
The big dog		**The big dog** focuses on making sense of sentences through matching them to pictures and predicting the endings. Through this activity the children develop an awareness that sentences are about things which happen or exist. To prepare for it, the children could play a game in which they take turns to say what an animal or other character did, where, when or how. This could be linked with story-telling.		200
Sentence factory		**Sentence factory** develops skills in writing short, simple sentences. You could also make 'lift-the flap' sentence boards for the children to use in creating sentences.		201
Silly sentences		**Silly sentences** provides a game in which the children can use and develop their understanding of sentences. Draw out that the words of a sentence must make sense but that it can be about something silly. As an extension activity you could ask the children questions which lead to the formation of sentences: for example, 'Who?', 'What did he/she/it do?', 'Where?' (or 'When?' or 'How?'). This can be varied so that on some occasions the sentences can be silly but on others they must be sensible.		202
The park		**The park** and **Zoo time** focus on writing the ending of a sentence and then using the first completed sentence as a model for others. It is useful to point out the capital letters and full stops. As a further extension activity some children could be asked to write sentences which begin 'I cannot see ...' or 'At the zoo there is no ...'.		203–204
Zoo time				
In the street		**In the street** and **On the beach** focus on writing a word in the middle of a sentence and then using the completed sentence as a model for writing others. This format could be used for writing about a place the children visit.		205–206
On the beach				
Treasure hunt		**Treasure hunt** and **Follow my leader** introduce the use of 'then' to start a sentence and develop the children's understanding of the purpose of this word. Before beginning Treasure Hunt they could follow a treasure trail around the classroom or playground and say what they found. The trail could be prepared beforehand, with arrow signs to guide the children. To prepare for Follow my leader, you could play the game, Follow my leader, with the children not only copying the leader's actions, but also saying what they are doing. Afterwards ask them what they did; after the first response they should respond with sentences beginning with 'Then'.		207–208
Follow my leader				
Along the street: 1 and 2		**Along the street: 1** and **2** together form a game which the children can play which leads to the writing of sentences beginning with 'Then'. They can look at the game board to help them to remember the sequence of the objects they saw. You could help the children to make a large floor mat in the form of the game board on which to record a real walk by drawing pictures in the correct order. They could then say and write sentences about their walk, using the floor mat (which could be covered with protective film) as a prompt. This could also be made available for free play activities.		209–210
I can tap, tap, tap		**I can tap, tap, tap** provides the starting point for an action song the children can make up. It develops their ability to form sentences. In the extension activity they can add actions such as 'bang', 'hum', 'kick', 'shake' and 'wobble'. They could sing the song so that the verses are incremental, which will require them to remember all the preceding actions.		211

Old Macdonald's farm	**Old Macdonald's farm** develops the children's ability to make up sentences containing the connective word 'and'. They might find this difficult if they had to write the entire sentence, but here they are required only to fill one or two gaps with words provided on the page. This could be linked with work in knowledge and understanding of the world (Science and Geography) involving a farm visit. An activity area could be set up containing a 'farm' with model animals, tractors, people and so on.	212
Mrs Snip	**Mrs Snip** helps the children to write sentences. They could first sing the song while performing the actions. In the extension activity they could add actions such as 'dye', 'shampoo', 'trim', 'curl', 'straighten', 'crimp'. This could be used to support work in a class 'hairdresser's corner' for role-play, which could be linked with mathematics (writing prices and bills).	213
Goldilocks	**Goldilocks** provides formats to help the children to write sentences about a character in a well-known story. They develop skills in considering the meaning of a sentence by predicting the missing words. They can then use the completed sentences as models for writing their own. You could provide similar sets of skeleton sentences about other stories they know.	214

How could you help?

- **Choose someone to help.**
- **Say how you would help them.**

Jack and Jill

Little Miss Muffet

Polly

Lucy Lockett

Mary

Humpty Dumpty

Three blind mice

Incey Wincey Spider

Old Mother Hubbard

The old woman who lived in a shoe

Little Boy Blue

Pussy

Teachers' note Cut out the cards and give one to each child or provide enough for a group to have a choice. The children could take turns to say which nursery rhyme character is on their card and what happened to him or her. This could involve saying or singing the rhyme (or part of it). Ask them to think of a way of helping the character.

A Lesson for Every Day
Literacy
4–5 Years
© A&C Black

Keep Grandma safe

- **How can Little Red Riding Hood's Grandma keep safe?**
- **Draw and write on the house.**
- **Phone and tell her what to do.**

You need

A play phone

NOW TRY THIS!

- **How could the other characters help Grandma to stay safe?**
- **Phone and tell one of them.**

Teachers' note Use this after reading the story of *Little Red Riding Hood*. Ask the children what happened to Grandma and ask them to think about what she could have done to stay safe. You could encourage 'thinking time' by asking them not to say their answer right away but to think about it.

A Lesson for Every Day
Literacy
4–5 Years
© A&C Black

The new baby

- **How does Deepak feel?**
- **Draw his face.**
- **What is Deepak thinking?**
- **Tell your group.**
- **Write in the speech bubble.**

NOW TRY THIS!

- **Think about something that happened in your family.**
- **Tell a partner about it.**

Teachers' note Begin with pictures of babies in the families of children in the class. Ask what they like about having a baby in the family and if there is anything they do not like. Those who have no younger siblings could say what they would like and dislike about having a baby in the family. Ask what differences the baby might make.

A Lesson for Every Day
Literacy
4–5 Years
© A&C Black

Moving house

- **How do the children feel?**
- **Draw their faces.**
- **What are they thinking?**
- **Tell your group.**
- **Write in the speech bubbles.**

NOW TRY THIS!

- **What do you think about moving house?**
- **Tell a partner about it.**

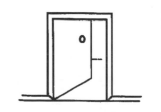

Teachers' note The children could begin by talking to a friend about the picture. As they do so you could ask open questions: *What are these two people doing? Why do you think they are doing that? What do you think is happening in the house? What might happen next?*

A Lesson for Every Day
Literacy
4–5 Years
© A&C Black

I can draw a house

- **Finish the house.**
- **Colour it.**
- **Tell a friend about the house.**

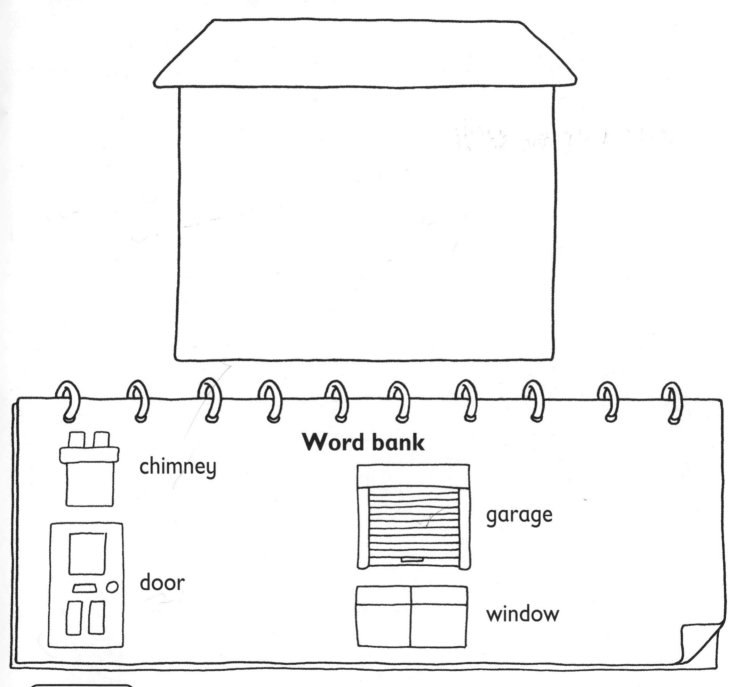

Word bank

chimney

door

garage

window

NOW TRY THIS!

- **Who lives in this house? Tell your friend about them.**

Teachers' note First ask the children to name the parts of the house in the drawing and in the word bank. Talk about whether all houses have all these, taking into account bungalows, flats and mobile homes. When talking about their drawings, the children can mention the number of doors and windows, whether the house has a chimney and what this is for, and so on.

A Lesson for Every Day
Literacy
4–5 Years
© **A&C Black**

Phone a friend

You want to ask your friend to come for tea.
- **Write what you will say.**
- **Write what your friend might say.**

When?
What time?

_____

_____

_____

_____

_____

_____

NOW TRY THIS!
- **Phone your friend.**
  Ask them to come for tea.

30

Teachers' note The children first need opportunities to have conversations with friends using 'play' phones. Discuss what they say when they phone someone or answer the phone. Ask them to think about what they might say to invite a friend for tea. They should plan what to say and write it in any way they can before having the conversation in pairs (using a phone as a prop, if possible).

A Lesson for Every Day
Literacy
4–5 Years
© A&C Black

Sally go round the Sun

- ## Say the rhyme.

Sally go round
the Sun,

Sally go round
the moon.

Sally go round
the chimney pots

On a Saturday
afternoon.

- ## Learn the rhyme.

Look and read

Cover

Say

Check

NOW TRY THIS!

- ## Make up some actions for the rhyme.

Teachers' note Read the rhyme to the children, then invite them to join in as you repeat it. Next, miss out words for the children to supply, especially 'Sun', 'Moon' and 'afternoon'. Draw out that the rhyme was written for fun and is not something that could really happen. After the children have had a chance to practise the rhyme, invite volunteers to recite it to the class, with actions.

A Lesson for Every Day
Literacy
4–5 Years
© A&C Black

Twinkle, twinkle, little star

- **Fill in the gaps.**
- **Say the rhyme.**

Word bank

are   high   sky

star   up

Twinkle, twinkle, little _____ ,

How I wonder what

you _____ !

_____ above the world

so _____ ,

Like a diamond in the _____ .

NOW TRY THIS!

- **Learn the rhyme.**

 Look and read   **Cover**   **Say**   **Check**

- **Record it**

32   **Teachers' note** Show the children the activity sheet and ask them if they know which nursery rhyme it is. Children who cannot read the words can use the picture as a cue. Invite volunteers to recite or sing the rhyme and to supply the missing words. Tape recorders will be needed for the extension activity. The children should listen to one another's recordings.

A Lesson for Every Day
Literacy
4–5 Years
© A&C Black

Action words

scramble and stumble	splish and splash	swish and swash
slide and glide	creep and crawl	crunch and scrunch
tumble and fumble	climb and clamber	wibble and wobble
duck and dodge	jump and jitter	scratch and scrape

Teachers' note Use this with 'Action places'. The cards can be used with a large group (up to 24, or more if some children share a card), ideally in a large space such as the hall or playground. Match the Action words to the Action places (the cards are in an appropriate order on each page) and read them out.

A Lesson for Every Day
Literacy
4–5 Years
© A&C Black

Action places

across the rocks

through the stream

through long grass

along the ice

through the tunnel

on the gravel

down the hill

over the wall

on the
stepping stones

under the branches

through the nettles

through the
brambles

A Lesson for Every Day
Literacy
4–5 Years
© A&C Black

Sounds and words

- **Say the words.**
- **Write the missing word.**
- **Say the sentence.**

Make it sound like the meaning.

I'm a stumbling grumbling

_____ .

snail

I'm a flitting fluttering

_____ .

crab

I'm a scuttling scrabbling

_____ .

hippopotamus

I'm a slipping sliding

_____ .

butterfly

NOW TRY THIS!

- **Do the actions and say a sentence for**

a worm

Teachers' note Read the first line aloud so that it sounds as if you are 'stumbling and grumbling' and ask the children to complete it with an animal, also doing the actions. They can then join in the next line and complete it, enact it and so on.

A Lesson for Every Day
Literacy
4–5 Years
© A&C Black

I like this word

- **Listen to the words.**
- **Say the words.**
- **Write your favourite word on the flag.**

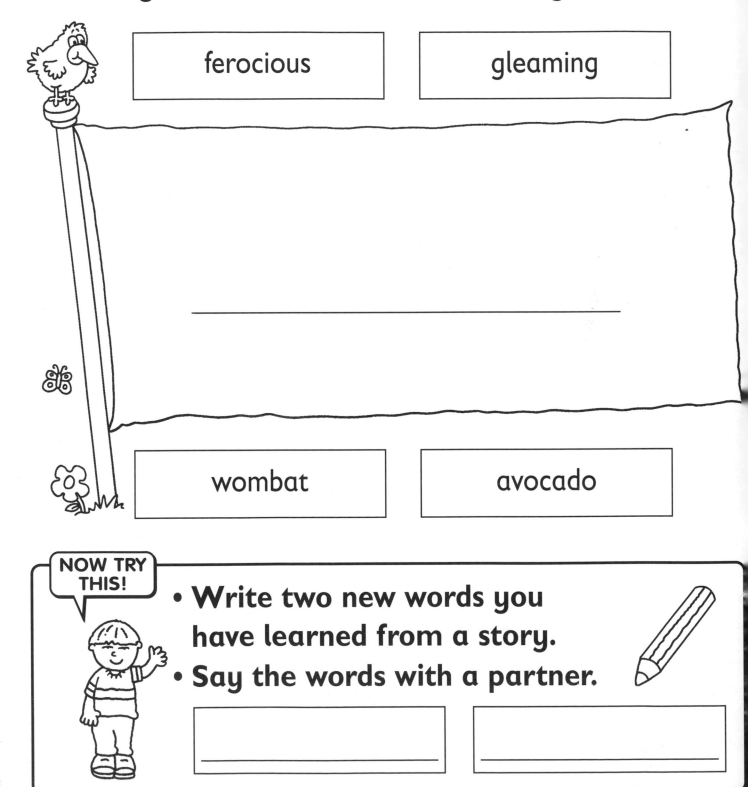

ferocious

gleaming

_____

wombat

avocado

NOW TRY THIS!

- **Write two new words you have learned from a story.**
- **Say the words with a partner.**

Teachers' note Read the first word to the children and invite them to repeat it. *Has anyone heard it before? Where? Do they know what it means?* You could use it in a sentence to demonstrate its meaning. Repeat this for the other words and let the children choose their favourite word.

A Lesson for Every Day
Literacy
4–5 Years
© A&C Black

Whisky frisky: 1

• Say the poem.

Whisky frisky,
Hipperty hop,
Up he goes
To the tree top!

Whirly, twirly,
Round and round,
Down he scampers
To the ground.

Furly, curly,
What a tail,
Tall as a feather,
Wide as a sail.

Where's his supper?
In that shell.
Snap! Crack!
Out it fell.

Anonymous

• Learn the poem.

Look and read **Cover** **Say** **Check**

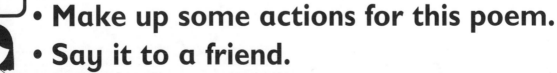

NOW TRY THIS!

• Make up some actions for this poem.
• Say it to a friend.

Teachers' note Read the poem to the children and ask them what kind of animal it could be about and why they think this is. (See also 'Whisky frisky: 2'.) Ask them what they think the animal's supper was. Again, they should explain their answers. Tell the children that acorns are poisonous to humans. You could do this part of the activity during a PE lesson and ask the children to move around as if they were the animal.

A Lesson for Every Day
Literacy
4–5 Years
© A&C Black

Teachers' note Use this with 'Whisky frisky: 1'. If the children cannot work out what the animal in the poem is, show them this page as a clue. Photocopy it onto thick paper or thin card. Ask them to cut out the squirrel, and help them to tape it onto a stick or a length of thick card. As you read the poem encourage them to move it around in the way described.

A Lesson for Every Day
Literacy
4–5 Years
© A&C Black

Way down south

- **Say the rhyme.**
- **Change the animals.**
- **Say your new rhyme.**

Way down south

Way down south where bananas grow,

A grasshopper stood on an elephant's toe.

The elephant said, with tears in his eyes,

"Pick on somebody your own size."

butterfly	ladybird	
hippo	donkey	

NOW TRY THIS!

- **Make up a new first line for the rhyme.**

Way down south where _____ grow.

Teachers' note Help the children to repeat this rhyme with expression and discuss why you are doing this, making them aware of the use of expression. Once they know it, cut out the animal cards and give one to each child (duplicate for larger groups than six) and ask them to make up a verse for their animal and say it in the same way.

A Lesson for Every Day
Literacy
4–5 Years
© A&C Black

Merry Mr Cherry

Over the hill and along the lane

Went merry Mr Cherry wearing a beret.

And nosey Miss Rosie carrying a posy.

And Mike MacTyke riding a bike.

And thin Mr Finn pushing a bin.

And the two Miss Tates on roller skates.

NOW TRY THIS!

- **Make up another verse for the rhyme.**
- **You could begin:**

  and big Mr Fig ...
- **Say the rhyme with a partner.**

Teachers' note Read the introductory rhyme with the children and tell them that what follows is a rhyme about the people who join merry Mr Cherry on his walk. Re-read it, omitting *beret* and invite the children to supply the missing word. Repeat this for each verse. Invite them to repeat the entire rhyme. Some children could add to it.

A Lesson for Every Day
Literacy
4–5 Years
© A&C Black

Under the dark

- **Listen to the poem.**
- **Say the poem.**
- **Learn the poem.**

Sleeping outdoors

Under the dark
is a star.

Under the star
is a tree.

Under the tree
is a blanket.

Under the blanket
is me.

Marchette Chute

NOW TRY THIS!

- **Think of new words to fill the gaps.**
- **Say your new poem.**

Under the dark is _____.

Under the _____

is _____.

Teachers' note Remind the children of lively rhymes or poems they know, then read 'Under the dark' quietly, fairly slowly and in a gentle tone. Discuss the different expressions you used in the different kinds of poem.

A Lesson for Every Day
Literacy
4–5 Years
© A&C Black

Story characters: listen and tell

- **Listen to someone talking about a story character.**
- **Think who it might be.**
- **Check with your group, then tick the picture.** ✔

Cinderella

The Fairy Godmother

An Ugly Sister

The Prince

A Lizard

Red Riding Hood

The Woodcutter

Grandma

The Wolf

NOW TRY THIS!

- **Make another page like this with different story characters on it.**

Teachers' note Cut out the cards and use the ones the children will know. You could first remind them of the stories. Give a card to each child and ask them not to show it to the others. They can then take turns to tell the group about their character: the others have to guess who it is.

A Lesson for Every Day
Literacy
4–5 Years
© A&C Black

- **Tell a partner what you can see happening in the picture.**

- **Talk about what might be happening in Cinderella's house.**

NOW TRY THIS!

- **Tell a story about what another character in *Cinderella* might be doing.**

Teachers' note Use this activity after the children have heard or read the story of Cinderella. They could talk about the scene shown here, saying what they know has happened and what Cinderella is doing. Then ask them what might be happening in her house while she is out at the ball (who might be at home? What they might be doing and saying?)

A Lesson for Every Day
Literacy
4–5 Years
© **A&C Black**

Offstage: 2

- **Tell a partner what you can see happening in the picture.**
- **Talk about what the other Billy Goats Gruff might be doing.**

NOW TRY THIS!

- **Talk about why the Troll stays under the bridge.**

Teachers' note Use this activity after the children have heard or read the story of *The Three Billy Goats Gruff*. They could talk about the scene shown here, saying what they know has happened and what the Billy Goat and the Troll are doing and saying. Then ask them what the other Billy Goats might be doing and saying.

A Lesson for Every Day
Literacy
4–5 Years
© A&C Black

The three little pigs

- **Cut out the pictures.**
- **Put them in order.**
- **Tell the story to a partner.**

NOW TRY THIS!

- **Draw what happens next.**
- **Tell the end of the story.**

Teachers' note The children should first have listened to or read the story of *The Three Little Pigs*. They could work in pairs to put the pictures in order and retell the story.

A Lesson for Every Day
Literacy
4–5 Years
© A&C Black

Goldilocks story maze

- **Follow the maze.**
- **Colour things that were in the story of Goldilocks.**

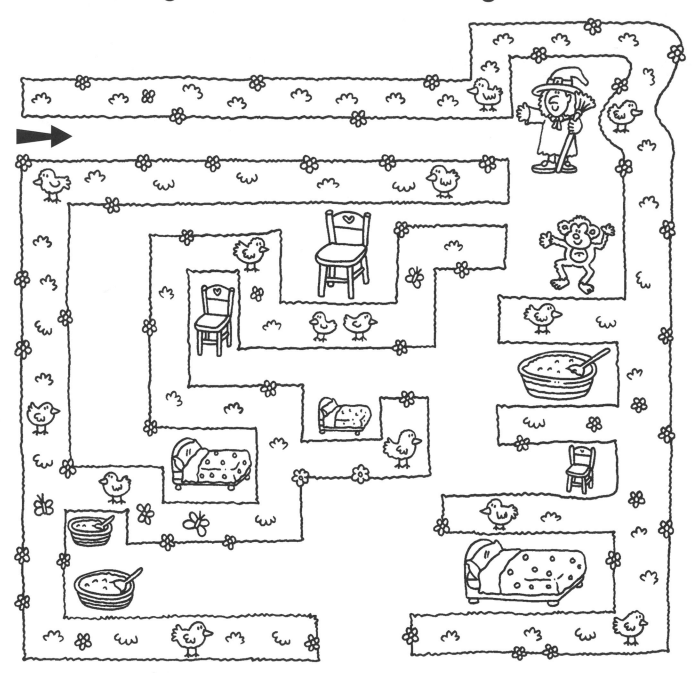

- **Tell a partner about one of the things in the story.**

Teachers' note The children should first have listened to or read the story of *Goldilocks and the Three Bears*. They could work in pairs or a small group, following the maze with a finger to find the way out and commenting on any character or object they encounter.

A Lesson for Every Day
Literacy
4–5 Years
© A&C Black

Partners

- Ask a partner about favourite things.
- Look at your partner.  Listen.
- Draw and write about your partner here.

	_____ likes this colour.
This is _____	_____
_____ likes this food.	_____ likes this _____.
_____	_____

NOW TRY THIS!

- **Tell someone else about your partner.**

Teachers' note The children should work on this in pairs. Read the first instruction with them and ask them to listen to a partner. Suggest some questions they could ask. They should then draw and write their report about the partner (who could then move on to another activity). They could swap roles during another lesson.

A Lesson for Every Day
Literacy
4–5 Years
© A&C Black

47

'What's in the road?

What's in the road, Mr Toad?
What can you see in the road?
In the road I can see a car
going fast and going far.

What's in the road, Mr Toad?
What can you see in the road?
In the road I can see two vans
and a car
going fast and going far.

What's in the road, Mr Toad?
What can you see in the road?
In the road I can see three bikes,
two vans
and a car
going fast and going far.

NOW TRY THIS!

- **Draw the next four things in the road.**
- **Say the rhyme with a partner.**

48

Teachers' note Read the first verse aloud to the children using two different 'voices' – one for the questioner and one for Mr Toad. Repeat it, missing out words such as road and far and encouraging the children to supply them. See the notes on the activity on page 9 for the second and third verses. (Use with 'Things in the road'.)

A Lesson for Every Day
Literacy
4–5 Years
© A&C Black

Things in the road

four jeeps

five diggers

six trucks

seven buses

eight tractors

nine lorries

ten horses

Teachers' note Use this with 'What's in the road' to extend the rhyme. Remind the children that they must listen to everything Mr Toad says so that they can say the same and add something else to it. They could collect pictures of other vehicles to add to the list and make a wall display to show what Mr Toad saw.

A Lesson for Every Day
Literacy
4–5 Years
© A&C Black

Six jolly sailors

- **Listen to the rhyme.**
- **Say the missing words.**
- **Write the missing words.**

Six jolly sailors,
Sailing on the sea
One took a dive
And then there were _____

_____ jolly sailors,
Sailing on the sea
One swam to the shore
And then there were _____

_____ jolly sailors,
Sailing on the sea
One broke his knee
And then there were _____

NOW TRY THIS!

- **Make up the next three verses.**
- **Say them with a partner.**

Teachers' note Read the rhyme aloud to the children and encourage them to supply the missing words. You could then repeat it using actions: hold up fingers for each number, use a hand mime for sailing on the sea, took a dive, swam ashore and broke his knee.

A Lesson for Every Day
Literacy
4–5 Years
© A&C Black

Mrs Topping's shopping

cheese

milk

apples

grapes

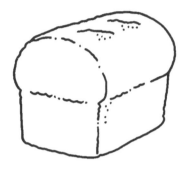

bread

sunflowers

coffee

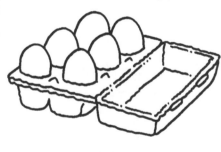

eggs

hat

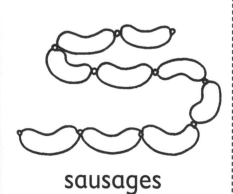

sausages

mop

gloves

Teachers' note With a group of eleven children (or omit pictures for smaller groups), begin by saying Mrs Topping once went shopping, Mrs Topping bought some cheese (hold up the picture), repeat this and invite one of the children to look at his or her picture and add what else Mrs Topping bought. Encourage them to use the words *a*, *an* or *some*, as appropriate.

A Lesson for Every Day
Literacy
4–5 Years
© A&C Black

Packed lunch: 1

- ## Work in a group.
- ## Choose four foods for the lunch box.

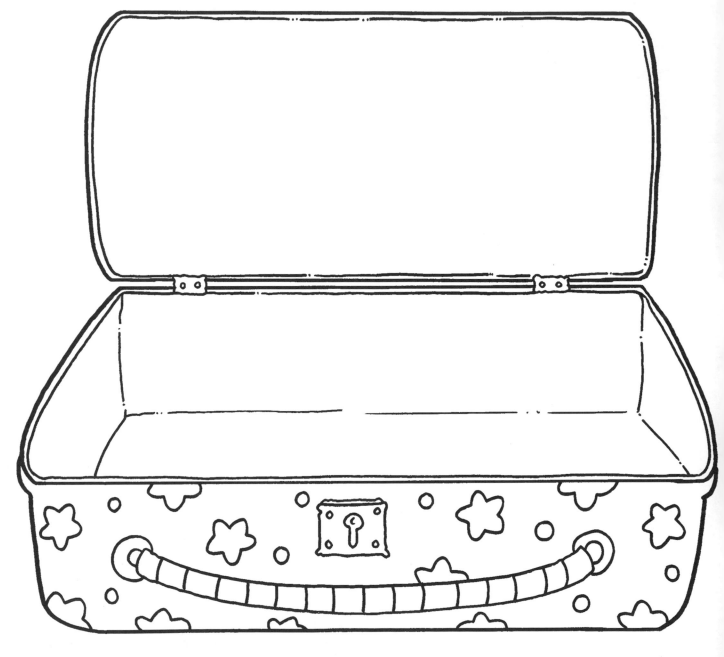

 **NOW TRY THIS!**

- ## Work with a partner.
- ## Draw and label four foods for a party.

Teachers' note Use this with 'Packed lunch: 2'. The children could work in groups of up to four. Cut out the pictures and spread them out on a table. Ask the children to take turns to pick up a picture and put it in the lunchbox. They should think about what is already in it and talk to their group about why they made this choice.

A Lesson for Every Day
Literacy
4–5 Years
© A&C Black

apple

banana

cake

cereal bar

cheese sandwich

chocolate

cola

crisps

lemonade

orange juice

pear

pizza

sausage roll

vegetable samosa

water

Teachers' note Encourage them to talk about their choices: for example, *There is already some fruit in the lunchbox, so I'm going to put a piece of pizza in it, There's some fruit and a piece of pizza in the lunchbox, so I'll put a drink in it: water because that's good for you.*

A Lesson for Every Day
Literacy
4–5 Years
© A&C Black

A day out

- **Work in a group.**
- **Plan a day out.**
- **Choose something from each set.**

NOW TRY THIS!

- **Tell another group about your plan.**

Teachers' note If the children work in a group of four they could each be allocated a set from which to choose something: a place to go, or an activity. They can then take turns to make up a story about a day out. Emphasise the importance of listening to those who are speaking, so that their part of the story will follow on.

A Lesson for Every Day
Literacy
4–5 Years
© A&C Black

Tell the way

- **Work with a partner.**
- **Choose a place to go.**
- **Draw a line to show the way.**
- **Tell another pair the way there.**

Start

NOW TRY THIS!

- **Find another way to the place you chose.**
- **Write the route.**

Teachers' note Show the children the starting point and read the word *Start*. Explain that they are going to choose a place to go, but not tell their friend which one, and then they will tell him or her how to get to it. They could first do this using a track chalked on the ground, with boxes or models to represent the places.

A Lesson for Every Day
Literacy
4–5 Years
© A&C Black

Sandcastles

- **Work with a partner.**
- **Put the pictures in order.**
- **Tell the story.**

NOW TRY THIS!

- **Draw pictures of something you and your partner did.**
- **Put them in order and say what you did.**

Work with your partner.

Teachers' note The children should cut out the pictures and try putting them in order, in discussion with a partner, and then saying, step by step, how the sandcastle was made. Ask them to check that this makes sense.

A Lesson for Every Day
Literacy
4–5 Years
© A&C Black

The best pencil-holder

- **Work with a group.**
- **Choose the best pencil-holder.**

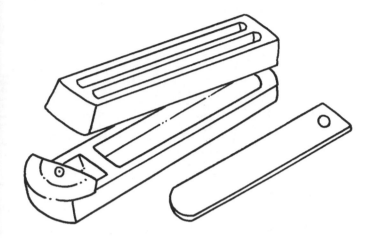

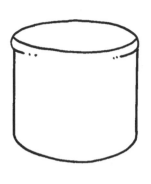

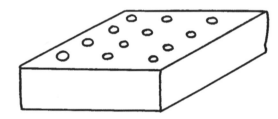

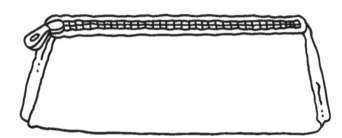

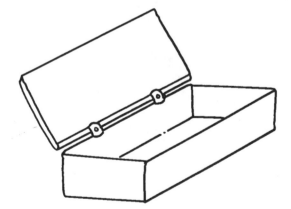

 **NOW TRY THIS!**

- **Draw how you could make a pencil-holder.**

 Work with a partner.

Teachers' note Ask the children to choose the pencil-holder they think is the best and to think about what makes it good. They should not tell their group until asked to. Once they have had time to think, invite them to tell their group which one they think is the best, and why. The others should listen and ask questions.

A Lesson for Every Day
Literacy
4–5 Years
© A&C Black

57

Shopping

- **Work with a group.**
- **What might each story character buy?** ✔
- **Draw lines to join them to their shopping.**

The Three Bears

Little Red Riding Hood

apples

rubber gloves

a bunch of flowers

porridge oats

Snow White

Cinderella

NOW TRY THIS!

- **Draw and write a shopping list for another story character.**

Work with a partner.

Teachers' note Ask the children to think about the Three Bears and to decide what they might need to buy. If they agree, one of them should draw the line to link the bears to the shopping (the children could take turns to do this). If they disagree, they should say why they think their choice is right and why another is wrong.

A Lesson for Every Day
Literacy
4–5 Years
© A&C Black

That's wrong!

- **What is wrong with this car?**
- **Work with a partner.**
- **Circle the wrong parts.**

NOW TRY THIS!

- **Ask another group what they think was wrong with the car.**

Teachers' note Encourage the children to take turns to point out a 'wrong' part and to say why it is wrong. They should ask if their friend agrees before circling it. Then it is the other child's turn. They should work together to check that they haven't missed anything.

A Lesson for Every Day
Literacy
4–5 Years
© A&C Black

Making things: actions

I made a ...

I made a ...

I made a ...

I made a ...

I made a ...

I made a ...

Teachers' note Use this with 'Making things'. Give each child a picture, ensuring that another child has the materials that match each object made. This activity is for up to twelve children: for smaller groups, remove a picture of an object and the corresponding picture of the materials.

A Lesson for Every Day
Literacy
4–5 Years
© A&C Black

Making things: materials

... with

... with

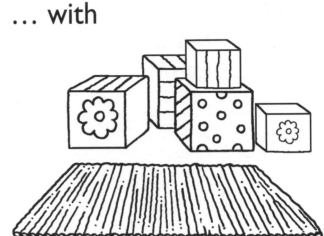

... with

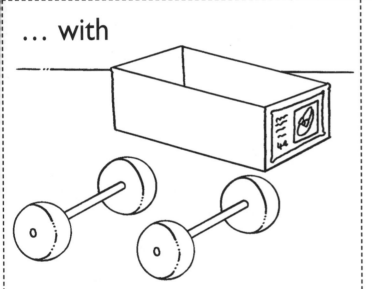

... with

... with

... with

Teachers' note Use this with 'Making things: actions'. Ask the children who have a picture of an object to read what it says on the card. Model how to complete the sentence. Then model how those with the pictures of materials should listen and then add to the sentence if they have the right card.

A Lesson for Every Day
Literacy
4–5 Years
© A&C Black

What's up the magic tree?

- **What will May find at the top of the magic tree?**
- **Draw and write on the tree.**
- **Tell a partner.**

NOW TRY THIS!

- **What will happen if May climbs the magic tree?**
- **Talk about it with a partner.**

Teachers' note The children could either make up their own story and then tell it to a friend (or to their group, or record it) or they could discuss the picture with a friend and make up a story together to tell to the others. They could draw a picture or write a few words to help them to tell the story ('so that you don't forget it').

62

A Lesson for Every Day
Literacy
4–5 Years
© A&C Black

Say what you know

- **Roll the die.**
- **Move your counter.**
- **Say something you know about the animal.**

You need

A die and a shaker

Four counters

START

FINISH

NOW TRY THIS!

- **Talk with a partner about one of the animals.**
- **Say what you have learned about it.**

Teachers' note Show the children how to play this game in a group of four, taking turns to roll the die, moving their counter the appropriate number of boxes along the track and then stopping and saying what the animal is and what they know about it.

A Lesson for Every Day
Literacy
4–5 Years
© A&C Black

63

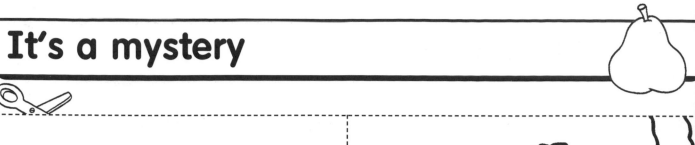

It's a mystery

It has no legs.	It has a shell.
It makes a slimy trail.	It eats plants.

64

Teachers' note Cut out the cards and ask the children to work in pairs to put them together to make a picture. Once the picture is correct they could glue it onto a piece of paper. *What is it?* They could work together to spell rabbit. Children trying the extension activity might need help in reading the cards. This can be used in different ways (see Notes on the activities page 10).

A Lesson for Every Day
Literacy
4–5 Years
© A&C Black

What are they like?

- ## What are these people like?
Talk to your group about them.

NOW TRY THIS!

- ## Who is your favourite person on this page?
- ## Tell a partner why.

Teachers' note Cut out the cards and give one to each pair of children. Ask them to talk about the person in the picture and to decide what he or she is like. Invite feedback and encourage the others to listen and ask questions such as *How can you tell she is friendly? What makes you think he is mean?*

A Lesson for Every Day
Literacy
4–5 Years
© **A&C Black**

What's the story?

- **What are these people doing?**
- **Talk to a partner.**

- **Choose a picture.**
- **Tell a partner what has happened.**
- **Say what might happen next.**

Teachers' note Cut out the cards and give one to each pair of children. Ask them to talk about what is happening in the picture and to tell the story of the picture. They could give the people names and say what might happen next. They could tell their stories to the others or record them.

A Lesson for Every Day
Literacy
4–5 Years
© A&C Black

Zoo plan: 1

Work in a group.
Choose four animals to share this pen in the zoo.

NOW TRY THIS!

• **Talk to another group about your zoo.**

eachers' note Use this with 'Zoo plan: 2'. The children could work in groups of up to four. Cut out the ictures and spread them out on a table. Ask the children to talk about which animals could live in the en and which ones could not, and why (for example, a lizard could not because it would be able to scape).

A Lesson for Every Day
Literacy
4-5 Years
© A&C Black

Zoo plan: 2

chimpanzee

donkey

giraffe

goldfish

hippo

lion

lizard

octopus

polar bear

python

seal

shark

tarantula

tiger

zebra

Teachers' note Use this with 'Zoo plan: 1'. The children should discuss which animals can live together, and why, and then take turns to pick up a picture and put it in the pen. The others should watch and listen and, if this animal could not live there, they should say so.

A Lesson for Every Day
Literacy
4–5 Years
© A&C Black

Toy story

- **Pretend you are one of these toys.**
- **Tell the story of your day.**

NOW TRY THIS!

- **What if two of the toys met one day?**
- **Tell the story.**

Teachers' note The children could name the toy they choose and talk to a friend about the toy's day. Ask questions such as *What happened when he woke up? What did she have for breakfast?* Invite responses such as *I wonder how he got that mark on his foot? I wonder who her friends are? I wonder how he knows when it's bed-time?*

A Lesson for Every Day
Literacy
4–5 Years
© A&C Black

Postman's knock

- **What are they saying?**
- **Say the words.**
- **Write in the speech bubbles.**

NOW TRY THIS!

- **Knock on a door.**
- **Your partner opens the door.**
- **What do you both say?**

Teachers' note The children should first have had experience of conversations with people who knock on the door of a pretend house: for example, those delivering milk or mail, neighbours, family members. Ask what they say when they meet someone they know and introduce phrases such as *Good morning, Good afternoon, Good evening, How are you?, Have a good day.*

A Lesson for Every Day
Literacy
4–5 Years
© **A&C Black**

The plaster cast

- **What might have happened?**
- **Talk with a partner.**
- **Write on the plaster and the sling.**
- **Tell your group.**

NOW TRY THIS!

- **Think of some questions you could ask the girl in the picture.**
- **Tell a partner about it.**

Teachers' note Discuss injuries the children have had, especially if these led to a cast, sling or other treatment. Encourage them to add detail to responses such as *I had a sore arm, I sprained my ankle, I went to hospital* by asking *Which part of your arm? What were you doing when you hurt yourself? What happened at the hospital?*

A Lesson for Every Day
Literacy
4–5 Years
© A&C Black

At the dentist's

- **What is happening?**
- **Talk with a partner.**
- **Write in the box.**
- **Tell your group.**

NOW TRY THIS!

- **Think about when you went to the dentist.**
- **Tell a partner about it.**

Teachers' note You could set up a mock dentist's surgery in the classroom for role-play using a reception desk, appointments book, dentist's chair and mirrors (no implements for poking in mouths). Encourage the receptionist and dentist to greet their patients, talk about their treatment and say *Goodbye, see you in six months* and so on.

A Lesson for Every Day
Literacy
4–5 Years
© A&C Black

Mr Dingle's day

- **Follow the story map.**
- **Tell the story of Mr Dingle's day.**

NOW TRY THIS!

- **Draw a story map for your day.**
- **Tell a partner about it.**

Teachers' note The children could use this page in pairs or groups of three or four, taking turns to talk about each picture. Encourage them to use sequential language by asking questions such as *What did Mr Dingle do first? Then what did he do? What did he do next? What did he do after that?*

A Lesson for Every Day
Literacy
4–5 Years
© A&C Black

The tower

- **Put the pictures in order.**
- **Say what happened.**

- **Change the last picture.**
- **Make it a happy story.**

74

Teachers' note Cut out the pictures and give them to the children to put in order, working with a partner. They should agree about which picture comes first, second and so on. One pair could tell the story to the others, who could ask questions. Model some questions: *What made both children happy? What do you think happened to the tower?*

A Lesson for Every Day
Literacy
4–5 Years
© **A&C Black**

Finger puppets

- **Work in a group.**
- **Cut out the puppets.**
- **Act the story.**

Goldilocks

Goldilocks and the Three Bears

Father Bear

Mother Bear

Baby Bear

NOW TRY THIS!

- **Change the story.**
- **Make up another character.**

Teachers' note The children should work in groups of four. Photocopy this page onto card for each group. Help them to cut out the finger holes (by folding them into semi-circles before cutting). Each child should then wear a finger puppet as the group enacts the story. They might need help in finding a fair way to allocate the roles.

A Lesson for Every Day
Literacy
4–5 Years
© A&C Black

Billy goat mask

- **Cut out the mask.**
- **Act the story.**

Teachers' note Use this with 'Troll mask'. Photocopy these pages onto card. The children should work in groups of four; each group will need three billy goat masks, one troll mask and eight elastic bands. The children should colour the masks, making each one slightly different, before they cut them out.

Troll mask

- **Cut out the mask.**
- **Act the story.**

Teachers' note Use this with 'Bily goat mask'. Use a hole puncher to make holes in the shaded circles, then loop an elastic band through each hole. The children should wear the masks (with the elastic loops over their ears) as they enact the story.

A Lesson for Every Day
Literacy
4–5 Years
© A&C Black

77

The little red hen

• **Write the words.**

The little red hen

The cat

The pig

The dog

• **Work in a group.**
Act the story.

NOW TRY THIS!

• **What happens next?**
Act the rest of the story.

Teachers' note Read the traditional tale of *The Little Red Hen* to the class. Discuss what the little red hen asks each character ('Who will help me?') and what they reply ('Not I'). These words should be written in the speech bubbles. Then put the children into groups of four and help them to allocate the parts for acting the story.

A Lesson for Every Day
Literacy
4–5 Years
© A&C Black

Characters and words

• **Join the characters to the words.**

Fee, fi, fo, fum

Mirror, mirror on the wall

The Gingerbread
Man

The Wicked
Queen

The Three Bears

The Giant

Run, run as fast as
you can!

Who's been sitting
in my chair?

**NOW TRY
THIS!**

• **What did they say?**

The Troll

The Wolf

Teachers' note Invite volunteers to talk about what the story characters did and what happened to them. They could then read what the characters said. Many children will know the words without being able to read them. For the extension activity, make sure the children are familiar with the catch-phrases from *The Three Billy Goats Gruff* and *The Three Little Pigs*.

A Lesson for Every Day
Literacy
4–5 Years
© A&C Black

Jack goes to market

Jack goes to market to sell his mother's cow.

- **Choose a picture for the story. Tick it.**
- **Draw and write what happens next.**

 **NOW TRY THIS!** • **Tell your new story about Jack.**

Teachers' note First read the story of Jack and the Beanstalk with the children and talk about the idea of swapping a cow for a handful of beans (see page 12). Help them to read these alternative versions and allow time for discussion before they choose one. Ask them if they think the swaps on this page would be good for Jack. Might the parrot or the old car have hidden magical qualities?

A Lesson for Every Day
Literacy
4–5 Years
© A&C Black

Story groups: 1

I am going to see Grandma.

Who has been sitting on my chair?

I eat little boys.

I eat grandmas.

My chair is broken.

I'll swap these beans for your cow.

Teachers' note Use this with 'Story groups: 2'. The cards depict characters from four different stories. Make enough copies of the pages for each child to have one card. Introduce the term character and give out the cards (you could omit a character from each story if necessary). Some children might need to discuss their character with an adult helper.

A Lesson for Every Day
Literacy
4–5 Years
© A&C Black

Teachers' note Help the children to identify the story the character comes from, then ask them to imagine they are the character and think about how they might feel. Encourage them to find the other characters from their story among the children in the class. As they find a character from their story they should enact parts of it together until they find the others.

A Lesson for Every Day
Literacy
4–5 Years
© **A&C Black**

Alphabet action song

Draw actions to match the letters .

A

A makes me ask for an apple in the night

B makes me bite it with a great big bite

C makes me click with a thumb and a finger

C

D makes me dance to the song of the singer

E makes me elbow left and right all day

F makes me fly far away, far away

N

G makes me give a gift of gold

H makes me hold – hold, hold, hold

E

I makes me itch – itch all day

J makes me jump and jog away

K makes my legs give a great big kick

O

L makes my tongue want to lick, lick, lick

M just tells me to make a mess

N makes me nod – nod to say yes

S

O makes me offer you an orange drink

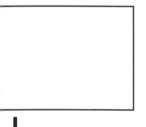

I

P makes me pull out the plug from the sink

Q makes me quick in everything I say

R makes me run in a race today

U

S makes me sing a song of the sea

T makes me tap – tap, tap on my knee

U makes me undo an umbrella in the rain

V makes me visit Auntie Jane

L

W makes me walk along, along, along

X makes me x-ray to find out what is wrong

X

Y makes me yell to you, you, you

Z makes me zoom around the zoo.

eachers' note Use the name of the letter at the start of each line – not the phoneme it represents.
ntroduce the rhyme a section (perhaps four lines) at a time. Say or sing it (to any suitable tune). As
ou say or sing each line, demonstrate the action and invite the children to repeat the line and join in.
se an alphabet frieze at the same time to remind the children what the letters look like.

A Lesson for Every Day
Literacy
4–5 Years
© A&C Black

Start the same

- **What is in the bag?**
- **Say the** words .
- **Write the first** letter .

p	n	m	d

NOW TRY THIS!

- **Draw something beginning with** m .

Teachers' note Use this once the consonant phonemes /t/, /p/, /n/, /m/ and /d/ have been taught. Ensure that the children know the names of the objects; if necessary you could emphasise the initial sound as you say them. The children can then identify and write the letter each one begins with. The emphasis is on the initial consonant; the words should not be written in full.

A Lesson for Every Day
Literacy
4–5 Years
© A&C Black

Odd one out

Say the words for the pictures.

Listen to the first sounds .

Circle the odd one out in each set.

NOW TRY THIS!

• **Write the first letter .**

Teachers' note Use this once the consonant phonemes /**t**/, /**p**/, /**n**/, /**m**/ and /**d**/ have been taught. Ensure that the children know the names of the objects; if necessary you could emphasise the initial sound as you say them. The children can then identify and write the letter each one begins with. The emphasis is on the initial consonant; the words should not be written in full.

A Lesson for Every Day
Literacy
4–5 Years
© A&C Black

Missing a

- **Write** a **in the gap.**
- **Say the** sounds **.**
- **Say the** word **.**

s | t

p | | t

n | | p

p | | n

NOW TRY THIS!

- **Make another word with these.**
- **Say the sounds.**
- **Say the word.**

Teachers' note Use this once the vowel phoneme /a/ has been taught and the children have used phoneme frames (see notes on the activities on page 13). They could sound the completed words with a partner and then blend the phonemes to say the words. As a further extension, some children could make their own personal lists of words with **a** in the middle.

A Lesson for Every Day
Literacy
4–5 Years
© A&C Black

Missing i

- **Write** i **in the gap.**
- **Say the** sounds.
- **Say the** word.

p   n

s   t

t   p

n   p

NOW TRY THIS!

- **Write a word with**
- **Say the sounds.**
- **Say the word.**

i   s   p

Teachers' note Use this once the vowel phoneme /i/ has been taught and the children have used phoneme frames (see notes on the activities on page 13). They could sound the completed words with a partner and then blend the phonemes to say the words. As a further extension, some children could make their own personal lists of CVC words with **i** in the middle.

A Lesson for Every Day
Literacy
4–5 Years
© A&C Black

o in the middle

- **Say the** words **for the pictures.**
- **Listen for** o **.**
- **Colour the ones that have** o **in the middle.**

Teachers' note Use this once the vowel phoneme /o/ has been taught and the children have used phoneme frames (see notes on the activitiy on page 13). Ensure that they know the names of the objects in the pictures. They could repeat the words with a partner and listen for **o**. Instead of colouring the pictures with **o**, they could cut out and sort the pictures into sets (**o** and no **o**).

A Lesson for Every Day
Literacy
4–5 Years
© A&C Black

Llyfrgell Ganolog Caerdydd
Cardiff Central Library
02920382116

Customer name:
MEZHOUD, Louiza (Mrs)
Customer ID: ****4379

**Items that you have
borrowed**

Title: Al Qases Al Qir'ny
ID: 02967821
Due: 01 May 2018 23:59

Title: Tareekh al Arab fil Islam
ID: 01478670
Due: 01 May 2018 23:59

Title:
A lesson for every day : literacy
ages 4-5
ID: 02748217
Due: 01 May 2018 23:59

Title: Al Sufur wal Hijab
ID: 02259649
Due: 01 May 2018 23:59

Total items: 4
Account balance: £0.00
10 April 2018
Borrowed: 4
Overdue: 0
Hold requests: 0
Ready for collection: 0

Thank you for using the 3M™
SelfCheck System.

Missing $\boxed{e}$

- **Write** $\boxed{e}$ **in the gap.**
- **Say the** $\boxed{\text{sounds}}$.
- **Say the** $\boxed{\text{word}}$.

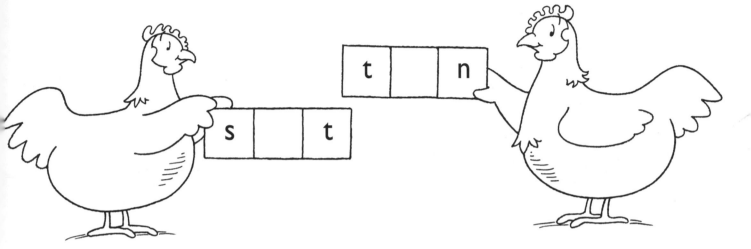

| s | | t |

| t | | n |

| p | | t |

| d | | n |

NOW TRY THIS!

- **Write the words.**

Teachers' note Use this once the vowel phoneme /e/ has been taught and the children have used phoneme frames (see notes on the activity on page 13). They could sound-talk the completed words with a partner and then blend the phonemes to say the words. You could also challenge them to look around the classroom, say the names of objects and listen for **e**: for example, *pen, desk, bell*.

A Lesson for Every Day
Literacy
4–5 Years
© A&C Black

Missing u

- **Write** u **in the gap.**
- **Say the** sounds .
- **Say the** word .

c [ ] t

s [ ] n

n [ ] t

m [ ] d

NOW TRY THIS!

- **Make a word with these.**
- **Say the sounds.**
- **Say the word.**

b g u

90

Teachers' note Use this once the vowel phoneme /u/ has been taught. (You could begin with the nursery rhyme *Rub-a-Dub-Dub, Three Men in a Tub*.) The children could sound-talk the completed words with a partner and then blend the phonemes to say the words. As a further extension, you could introduce some two-syllable words: for example, *suntan, mudbath, rucksack*.

A Lesson for Every Day
Literacy
4–5 Years
© A&C Black

The mill on the hill

- **Write** `ll` **in the gaps.**
- **Read the** `words` .

NOW TRY THIS!

- **Write the words.**

Teachers' note Use this once the consonant phoneme /l/ represented by the **ll** grapheme has been taught. Remind the children about 'two letters – one sound'. Point out that most short words that end with the **l** sound have **ll**. You could also make up sentences for the children to help you to spell: for example, *Fill the well*, *Tell Bill to sell the bell*, *Pull the bull to the dell*.

A Lesson for Every Day
Literacy
4–5 Years
© A&C Black

91

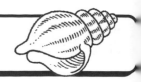

Names with ss

- **What are the animals' names?**
- **Write** ss **in the gaps.**
- **Read the** names .

| H | i | | |

| M | o | | |

| T | e | | |

| C | a | | |

| L | a | | |

| R | u | | |

| B | e | | |

NOW TRY THIS!

- **Write words that end with** ss .

| b | | |

| f | | |

| k | | |

Teachers' note Use this once the consonant phoneme /s/ represented by the **ss** grapheme has been taught. Remind the children about 'two letters – one sound'. Point out that most short words that end with the **s** sound have **ss** (also that one or two do not: for example, *gas* and *bus*). Useful two-syllable words and names for further extension activities include *buspass, fusspot, reckless*.

A Lesson for Every Day
Literacy
4–5 Years
© A&C Black

Letter change

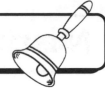

- **Read the** `word` .
- **Change the first** `letter` .
- **Read the new word.**

| m | a | d |

s →

| | a | d |

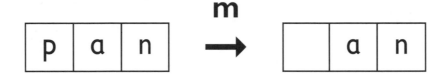

| p | a | n |

m →

| | a | n |

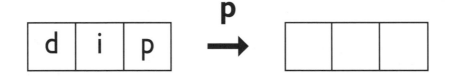

| d | i | p |

p →

| | | |

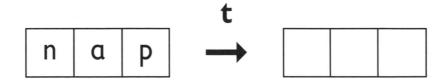

| n | a | p |

t →

| | | |

NOW TRY THIS!

- **Change the first letters to make new words.**

  pip   din   sit

Teachers' note Model the first example: ask the children to say the sound of each letter and then to put them together to make a word. Ask them what letter they should write in the gap in the next phoneme frame; they can then sound and read the new word. As a further extension activity they could try other letters at the beginning of the word: for example, *bad, dad, had, lad, pad.*

A Lesson for Every Day
Literacy
4–5 Years
© A&C Black

Missing v

- **Write** v **in the gap.**
- **Say the** sounds .
- **Say the** word .

| | e | t |

| | a | n |

| | a | t |

| | i | s | i | t |

NOW TRY THIS!

- **Write a boy's name that has** v **in it.**

Teachers' note Use this once the consonant phoneme /v/ has been taught. Explain that the animals visiting the vet's surgery have taken all the letters so the children need to write them back in on the signs. The children could sound the completed words with a partner and then blend the phonemes to say the words.

A Lesson for Every Day
Literacy
4–5 Years
© A&C Black

- **Write** $\boxed{x}$ **in the gap.**
- **Say the** $\boxed{\text{sounds}}$.
- **Say the** $\boxed{\text{word}}$.

f | o |

b | o |

m | i |

w | a |

f | i |

NOW TRY THIS!

- **Write a word for a number that ends with** $\boxed{x}$.

Teachers' note Use this once the consonant phoneme /**ks**/ has been taught. The children could sound-talk the completed words with a partner and then blend the phonemes to say the words. As a further extension, the children could begin personal or group collections of pictures, objects or activities whose names contain **x**: for example, *boxing, exercise, exit, hexagon, ibex, mixer, x-ray*.

A Lesson for Every Day
Literacy
4–5 Years
© A&C Black

Yan says yes

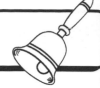

- **Help Yan the robot to speak.**
- **Write** $\boxed{y}$ **in the gaps.**
- **Say the** $\boxed{\text{sounds}}$.
- **Say the** $\boxed{\text{word}}$.

	e	s

	a	m

	a	p

Yan

	e	t

	u	m

	e	ll

NOW TRY THIS!

- **Think of a colour that begins with** $\boxed{y}$.
- **Say it.**
- **Colour Yan in.**

96

Teachers' note After introducing the /y/ phoneme, show the children this page and introduce them to Yan the robot. Explain that Yan can only say words that begin with **y** but he cannot say anything at the moment because the letters that start his words have gone missing. Ask the children to write **y** in the gaps to help Yan speak. They could then use a 'robot voice' to sound-talk and say the words.

A Lesson for Every Day
Literacy
4–5 Years
© A&C Black

Word writer: 1

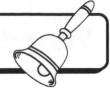

Say the words .
Say the sounds .
Write the words.

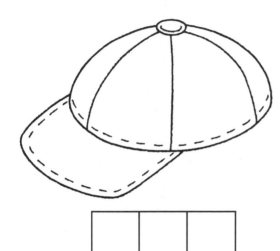

• **Make another word with**

Teachers' note Ask the children to say the word for the first picture. They could do this with a partner.
Then ask them to say it in 'sound-talk', sounding each letter. Model how to choose the correct letters
from the set on the fridge door and write each letter in the phoneme frame. Ensure that they know the
names of the other objects before they continue.

A Lesson for Every Day
Literacy
4-5 Years
© A&C Black

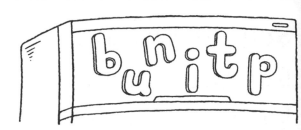

- **Say the** words .
- **Say the** sounds .
- **Write the words.**

Dog Food

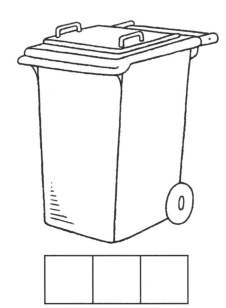

- **Make another word with**

Teachers' note Ask the children to say the word for the first picture. They could do this with a partner. Then ask them to say it in 'sound-talk', sounding each letter. Model how to choose the correct letters from the set on the fridge door and write each letter in the phoneme frame. Ensure that they know the names of the other objects before they continue.

A Lesson for Every Day
Literacy
4-5 Years
© A&C Black

Word writer: 3

Say the words .
Say the sounds .
Write the words.

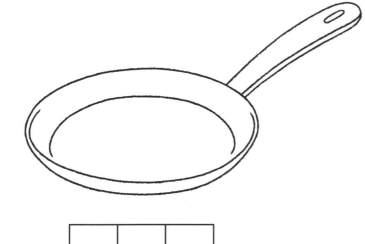

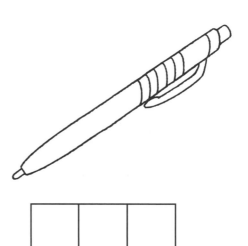

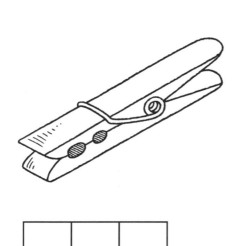

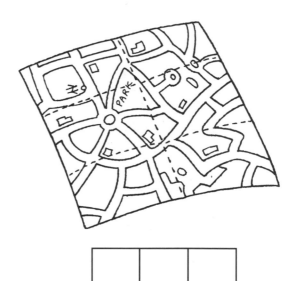

NOW TRY THIS!

• **Make a word with**

Teachers' note Ask the children to say the word for the first picture. They could do this with a partner.
Then ask them to say it in 'sound-talk', sounding each letter. Model how to choose the correct letters
from the set on the fridge door and write each letter in the phoneme frame. Ensure that they know the
names of the other objects before they continue.

A Lesson for Every Day
Literacy
4–5 Years
© A&C Black

Word writer: 4

- **Say the** words .
- **Say the** sounds .
- **Write the** letters .

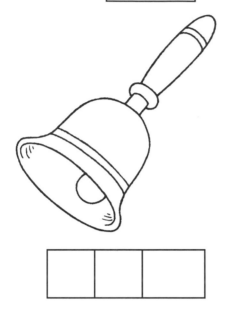

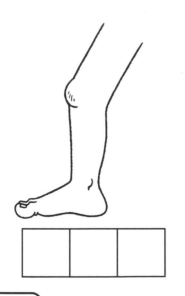

NOW TRY THIS!

- **Make another word with**

Teachers' note Ask the children to say the word for the first picture. They could do this with a partner. Then ask them to say it in 'sound-talk', sounding each letter. Model how to choose the correct letters from the fridge door and write each letter in the frame. Ensure that they know the names of the other objects before they continue. Remind them of 'two letters – one sound' for **ll**.

A Lesson for Every Day
Literacy
4–5 Years
© A&C Black

The king sings

The king likes to sing words with ng .
Write ng in the gaps.
- Say the sounds .
  Read the words .

b a

s o

h a

l o

th i

NOW TRY THIS!

- **Say the sounds. Write the word.**

Teachers' note Use this after teaching the /ng/ phoneme. Tell the children that the king likes to sing words that end with the same sound. What sound do they think that is? Ask them to say *king* and *sing* and listen for the sound at the end of both words. Also introduce two-syllable words with **ng** in the middle (see notes on the activity on page 14).

A Lesson for Every Day
Literacy
4–5 Years
© A&C Black

101

Cats and mice

- **Help the cats to catch a mouse to make a** `word`.
- **Write the** `letter` **in the gap.**
- **Read the word.**

ar | m

ar | k

 p

 h

 c

 y

ar | t

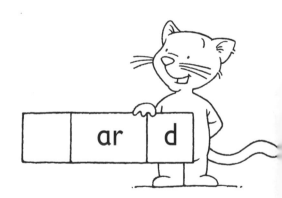

ar | d

NOW TRY THIS!

- **Write a letter in the gap to make a real word.**
- **Read the word.**

b | ar |

Teachers' note Use this after teaching the /**ar**/ phoneme. Tell the children that the cats need to catch mice that have a letter to fill the gap in their word. They should then try each letter in turn (without writing it) and say the word. Some children might first need to make the words, using magnetic letters. Also introduce two-syllable words with the **ar** sound: *carpet, darkness, starry.*

A Lesson for Every Day
Literacy
4–5 Years
© A&C Black

Hens and eggs

- **Help the hens to find their egg to make a** word .
- **Write the** letters **in the gaps.**
- **Read the word.**

| p | | n |
| k | | p |

ai   igh   ee   ow

| d | | n |
| r | | t |

NOW TRY THIS!

- **Write a letter in the gap.**
- **Read the word.**

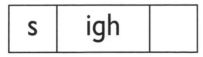

| s | igh | |

Teachers' note Use this after teaching the /ai/, /igh/, /ee/ and /ow/ phonemes. Tell the children that the hens need to find the eggs that have the letters to fill the gap in their word. They should then try each set of letters in turn (without writing them) and say the word. Some children might find it easier to make the words first, using magnetic letters.

A Lesson for Every Day
Literacy
4–5 Years
© A&C Black

Add and change: 1

- **Add a** boxed[sound] **to make a new** boxed[word].
- **Write the** boxed[letter].
- **Read the word.**

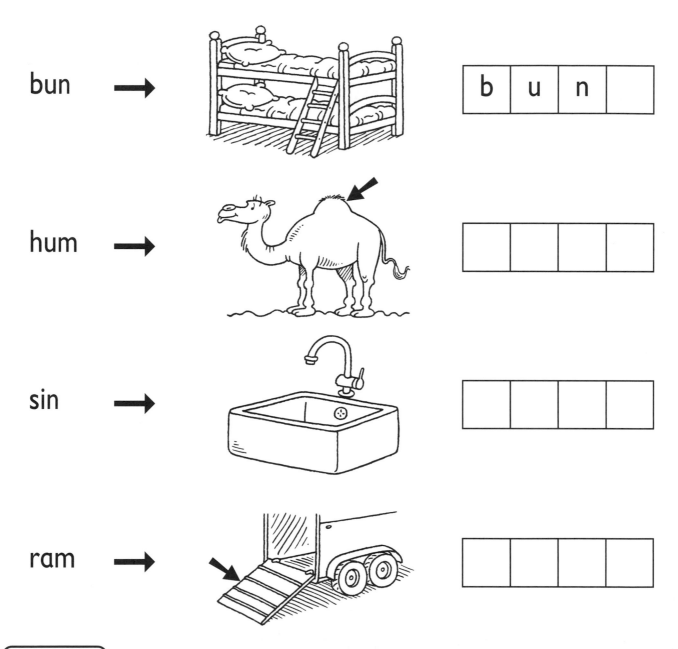

bun →

| b | u | n | |

hum →

| | | | |

sin →

| | | | |

ram →

| | | | |

NOW TRY THIS!

- **Add a letter to make a new word.**

| p | i | n | | | d | e | n | |

Teachers' note Ask the children to name and sound-talk the object in the first picture and then to check if the phoneme frame contains the correct letters. Ask what sound is missing at the end and which letter makes this sound. As a further extension, some children could change the last sound of a word to make a new word: for example, *bunk/bunch, hump/hums*.

A Lesson for Every Day
Literacy
4–5 Years
© A&C Black

Add and change: 2

- **Add a** `sound` **to make a new** `word` .
- **Write the** `letter` .
- **Read the word.**

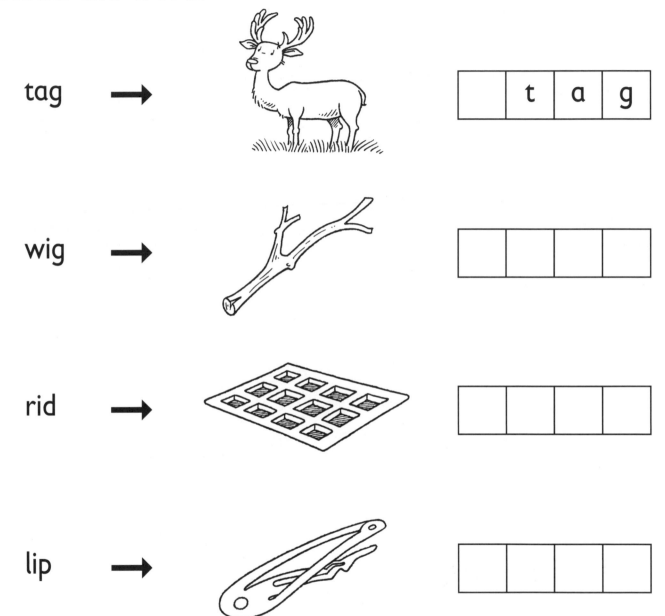

tag ➡️ | | t | a | g |

wig ➡️

rid ➡️

lip ➡️

NOW TRY THIS!

- **Add a letter to make a new word.**

| | n | i | p |

| | l | a | p |

Teachers' note Ask the children to name and sound-talk the object in the first picture and then to check if the phoneme frame contains the correct letters. Ask what sound is missing at the beginning and which letter makes this sound. As a further extension, some children could change the first sound of a word to make a new word: for example, *clip/slip*.

A Lesson for Every Day
Literacy
4–5 Years
© A&C Black

Teddy talk

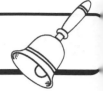

- **What is Teddy thinking of?**
- **Write the** word .

| n | e | | |

| p | | | |

| g | | | |

| m | | | |

NOW TRY THIS!

- **Write the word.**

| | | | |

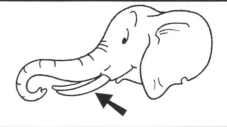

Teachers' note Ask the children to name and sound-talk the object in the first picture and then to check if the phoneme frame contains the correct letters. Ask which sounds are missing and which letters make these sounds. To make the activity either more or less challenging, delete or add letters before the children begin.

A Lesson for Every Day
Literacy
4-5 Years
© A&C Black

In the hat

- **Which things don't belong in the** ⃞h ⃞ **hat?**
- **Cross them out.** ⃞X⃞

NOW TRY THIS!

- **Say the names of three parts of your body that begin with** ⃞h⃞**.**
- **Draw pictures of them.**
- **Write** ⃞h⃞ **by each picture.**

Teachers' note Use this once the consonant phoneme /h/ has been taught. You could begin (orally only) with everyday words beginning with **h**: for example, *hello*, *help* and *hall*. Also make up silly sentences in which all the words begin with **h** (see notes on the activity on pages 15). Two-syllable words to introduce: *hatpin* and *humbug*.

A Lesson for Every Day
Literacy
4–5 Years
© A&C Black

In the bag

- **Which things don't belong in the** ☐b☐ **bag?**
- **Cross them out.** ☒

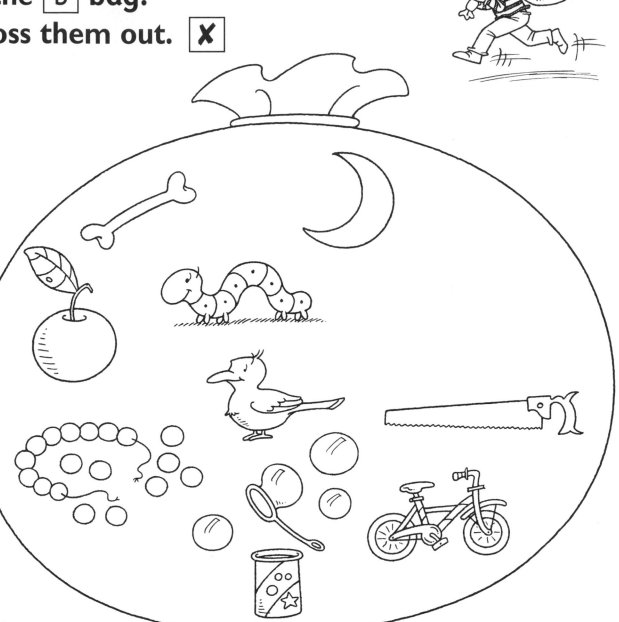

NOW TRY THIS!

- **Say the names of three animals that begin with** ☐b☐.
- **Draw pictures of them.**
- **Write** ☐b☐ **by each picture.**

Teachers' note Use this once the consonant phoneme /b/ has been taught. You could begin (orally only) with silly sentences in which all the words begin with **b** (see notes on the activity on page 15). As a further extension activity, introduce two-syllable words and names such as *backpack, bedbug, Batman, binbag, binman.*

A Lesson for Every Day
Literacy
4–5 Years
© A&C Black

On the fence

- **Which things don't belong on the ⬛ f fence?**
- **Cross them out.** ☒

NOW TRY THIS!

- Open a book.
- Look at the pictures.
- Name things that begin with ⬛ f .

Teachers' note Ask the children to take turns to point out and name something in the picture. The others should listen to the first sound and indicate if they hear **f** at the start of a word. As a further extension activity they could make up alliterative silly sentences about the objects that begin with **f**: for example, *Funny faces fetch four fish, Feet fall over fat fish, Forks find five flies.*

A Lesson for Every Day
Literacy
4–5 Years
© A&C Black

Looking for ⎣l⎦

• **Colour five things that begin with** ⎣l⎦**.**

NOW TRY THIS!

• **Look around your classroom.**
• **Draw three things that begin with** ⎣l⎦**.**
• **Say the** ⎣words⎦ **to a friend.**

Teachers' note Ask the children to take turns to point out and name something in the picture. The others should listen to the first sound and indicate if they hear **l** at the start of a word. As a further extension activity they could make up alliterative silly sentences about the objects that begin with **l**: for example, *Ladders like to laugh at lambs, A long log lingers in the lamplight.*

A Lesson for Every Day
Literacy
4–5 Years
© A&C Black

In the jar

Which things don't belong
in the $\boxed{j}$ jar?
Cross them out. $\boxed{\times}$

NOW TRY
THIS!

• Draw two other things to wear
that begin with $\boxed{j}$.

Teachers' note Use this once the consonant phoneme /j/ has been taught. You could begin (orally only) with silly alliterative sentences using words beginning with j: for example, jumping jellies jingle, ack's jazzy jumper jingles (also see notes on the activity page 15). Then say the words aloud with the children and ask them to say which things do not belong in the jar.

A Lesson for Every Day
Literacy
4–5 Years
© A&C Black

Wet wellies

- **Say the** words **.**
- **If they start with** w **, join them to the wet wellies.**

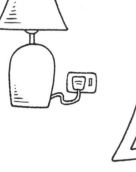 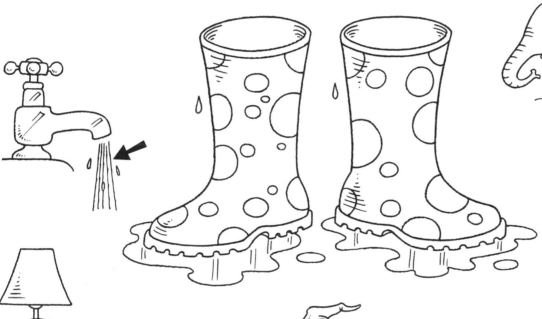 

NOW TRY THIS!

- **Write the** w **words.**

Teachers' note Use this once the consonant phoneme /**w**/ has been taught. You could begin (orally only) with silly sentences in which all the words begin with **w** (see notes on the activity on page 15). As a further extension activity, introduce two-syllable words and names such as *wigwam*, *cobweb*, *Tegwen*, *Anwen*.

A Lesson for Every Day
Literacy
4–5 Years
© A&C Black

Say the word **for each picture.**
Join it to the letter **it begins with.**

S   Z

NOW TRY THIS!

• **Write the word for**

Teachers' note Introduce the /z/ phoneme and give the children time to practise saying it. They could also practise making zigzag movements before they write the z. Ask them to name the objects in the pictures and to listen for z. Also remind them of the /s/ phoneme. Point out the line that joins the zebra to z and ask them to which letter they should join the sausages.

A Lesson for Every Day
Literacy
4–5 Years
© A&C Black

Sheena's ship

- **What belongs on Sheena's ship?** ☑
- **Say the** words .
- **Listen for** sh .

NOW TRY THIS!

- **Say the** sounds .
- **Write the word.**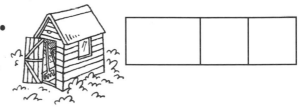

Teachers' note Tell the children that Sheena's ship is full of things beginning with the same sound. What sound do they think that is? Ask them to say 'Sheena's ship' and listen for the sounds they hear the most. They should then name the objects in the pictures and tick the boxes if they hear **sh**. You could also play an alliteration game about Sheena's ship (see notes on the activity on page 15).

A Lesson for Every Day
Literacy
4–5 Years
© A&C Black

Chuck's chat

Chuck only says words that have ch .
What does he say? ✔
Say the words.
Listen for ch .

NOW TRY THIS!

- Say the sounds .
- Write the word.

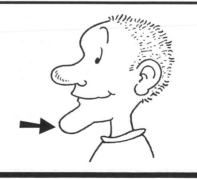

eachers' note Tell the children that Chuck likes words that begin with the same sound. What sound
o they think that is? Ask them to say 'Chuck's chat' and listen for the sounds they hear the most. They
hould then name the objects in the pictures and tick the boxes if they hear **ch**. You could also play an
lliteration game about Chuck's chat (see notes on the activity on page 15).

A Lesson for Every Day
Literacy
4–5 Years
© A&C Black

115

Find our foods

What do the children eat?
• Join each child to a food.

The words begin with the same letter.

 Emma

 Al

 Ruby

 Bob

 Tess

rice

eggs

toast

apples

bananas

NOW TRY THIS!

• Make up some silly things for the children to eat.

Start with the same letter as their name.

Teachers' note Explain that the children shown on the activity sheet like eating foods beginning with the first letters of their names. Ask the children what Emma eats and encourage them to make a sentence: *Emma eats eggs*. Let them complete the others, then invite feedback. For the extension activity, explain that the sentences need not make sense: for example, *Emma eats elephants*.

A Lesson for Every Day
Literacy
4–5 Years
© A&C Black

Slippery slimy

Are they slippery slimy? **or**

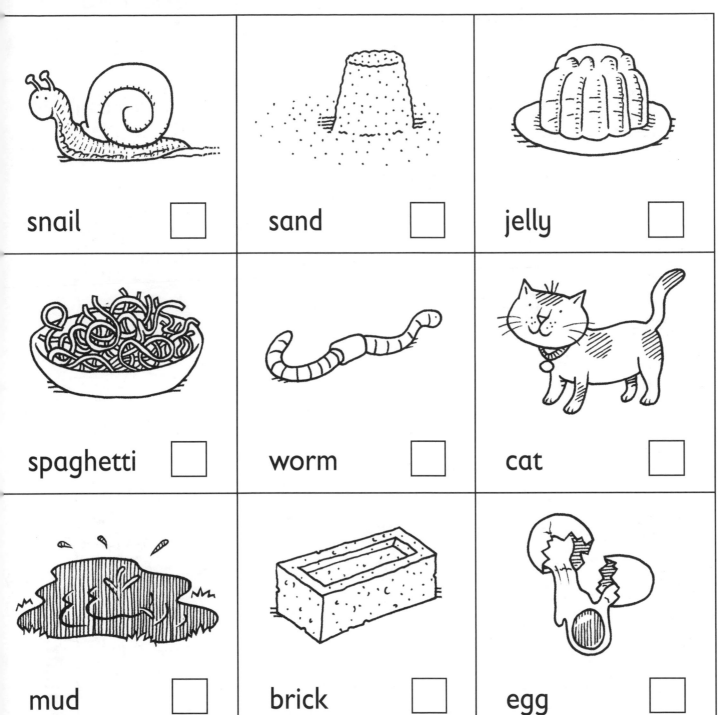

snail ☐	sand ☐	jelly ☐
spaghetti ☐	worm ☐	cat ☐
mud ☐	brick ☐	egg ☐

NOW TRY THIS!

- **Draw two other slippery slimy things.**
- **Write** labels .

Teachers' note Say the words *slippery slimy* and ask the children to repeat them. Do the words sound slippery and slimy? Compare them with words such as *crispy, crunchy, crackly*. Ask the children to decide whether each picture shows something slippery and slimy. Encourage them to say other 'slippery slimy' words: for example, *sloppy, slosh, slush, slap*. Point out the sound they begin with.

A Lesson for Every Day
Literacy
4–5 Years
© A&C Black

117

Flip, flap

- **Take turns to roll a dice.**
- **Move your counter.**
- **Look and read.**
  Does it go flip, flap?
- **Say** flip, flap **or** not flip, flap .

You need:
 a dice

8 8 4 counters

Start

washing — a big rock — wipers — a big ball — a tail — a chair — a cup — a flag — a wing — a block — a cake — a duster — long hair — a cat flap — a tap — an old boot

Finish

NOW TRY THIS!

- **Draw two other things that go** flip, flap .
- **Write** labels .

Teachers' note Split the class into groups of four. Each group will need a copy of this sheet, four counters and a dice. Introduce the activity by making 'flipping' or 'flapping' sounds using a piece of paper, a piece of cloth and some card or thin plastic. Then name the objects on the game board in turn, encouraging the children to call out 'flip, flap' or whisper 'Not flip, flap' as appropriate.

A Lesson for Every Day
Literacy
4-5 Years
© A&C Black

In the ring

Which things don't belong
in the ⬚r⬚ ring?

• Cross them out. ✗

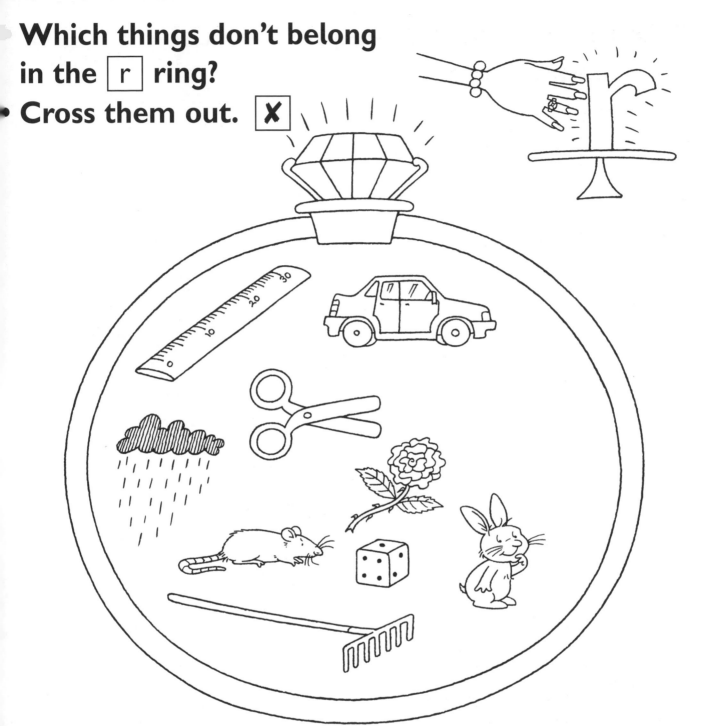

NOW TRY THIS!

• **Collect pictures of three things
beginning with ⬚r⬚.**
• **Write ⬚r⬚ by each picture.**
• **Say the ⬚words⬚ to a friend.**

Teachers' note Use this once the consonant phoneme /r/ has been taught. You could begin with a
'treasure hunt' for objects beginning with /r/. Give each child a bag in which to collect these: for
example, *rubber, ruler, ring, rose, ribbon, rag.* As a further extension activity, introduce two-syllable
words and names such as *rucksack, ragbag.*

Real words, wacky words: 1

- **Read the** | words | **. Are they real words?**
- **Join them to the book or the bin.**

| m e p |
| c a p |
| c u p |
| p u t |
| n u g |

Real words

Wacky words

| k i g |
| p o t |
| g a p |
| s e p |
| g a s |

NOW TRY THIS!

- **Use these** | letters | **to write two real words.**

| t | i | s |

| m | u | s |

Teachers' note The children should first be familiar with 'phoneme buttons' – also 'sound-talk' (see notes on the activity page 16). Model how to say the sounds, using actions: tapping a finger on the palm of your hand for each phoneme button so that the children sound-talk each phoneme before blending them to say the word. Is it a real word – should it go in the book or in the bin?

A Lesson for Every Day
Literacy
4–5 Years
© A&C Black

Real words, wacky words: 2

Read the words **. Are they real words?**
Join them to the book or the bin.

f a i r

g a i r

z e a r

c u r l

m u r n

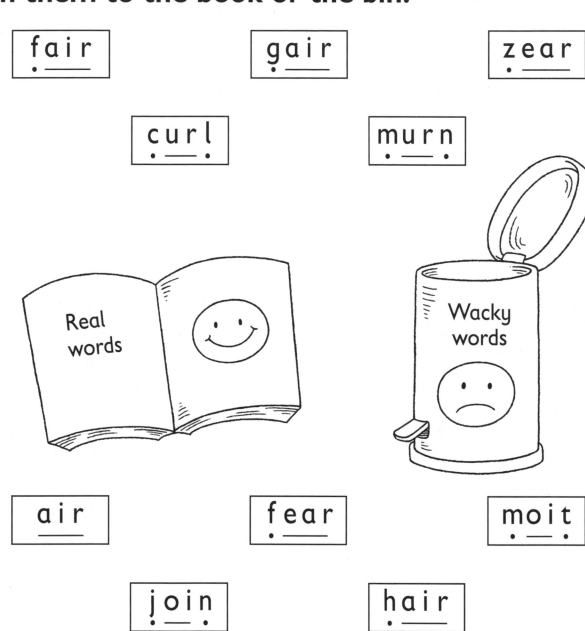

Real words

Wacky words

a i r

f e a r

m o i t

j o i n

h a i r

• **Use these** letters **to write two real words.**

| n | ur | t |

| air | p |

Teachers' note Remind the children how to say the sounds of the letters, using actions: tapping a finger on the palm of your hand for each phoneme button and 'drawing a line in the air' for each sound line so that the children say each phoneme in 'sound-talk' before blending them to say the word. Then ask if it is a real word – should it go in the book or in the bin?

A Lesson for Every Day
Literacy
4–5 Years
© A&C Black

121

Real words, wacky words: 3

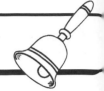

- **Read the**  . **Are they real words?**
- **Join them to the book or the bin.**

cowler

dinner

corner

farber

packer

Real words

Wacky words

murler

sarner

locker

curler

further

NOW TRY THIS!

- **Use these** 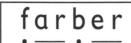 **to write two real words.**

| x | er | b | o | | er | i | ll | m |

Teachers' note Remind the children how to say the sounds of the letters, using actions: tapping a finger on the palm of your hand for each phoneme button and 'drawing a line in the air' for each sound line, so that the children say each phoneme in 'sound-talk' before blending them to say the word. Then ask if it is a real word – should it go in the book or in the bin?

A Lesson for Every Day
Literacy
4–5 Years
© A&C Black

Match-up: 1

• **Join the** words **to the pictures.**

f o r k

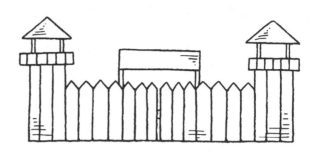

c u r l

c o r k

s u r f

f o r t

NOW TRY THIS!

• **Read the words with a friend.**

c h u r c h   n o r t h

Teachers' note Use this after teaching the /**or**/ and /**ur**/ phonemes. Ask the children to name the objects, listen for **or** and **ur** and join the words to the pictures. As a further extension, some children could replace the first or last letter of an **or** or **ur** word to make a new word (using selected letters, to avoid misspellings): for example, fork/pork/form, cork/corn/cord, surf/turf, fort/port.

A Lesson for Every Day
Literacy
4–5 Years
© **A&C Black**

• **Join the** words **to the pictures.**

coin

ear

oil

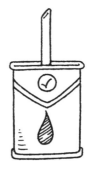

tear

earwig

NOW TRY THIS!

• **Read the words with a friend.**

gearbox   boiling

Teachers' note Use this after teaching the /oi/ and /ear/ phonemes. Ask the children to name the objects, listen for **oi** and **ear** and join the words to the pictures. As a further extension, some children could replace the first or last letter of an **oi** or **ear** word to make a new word (using selected letters, to avoid misspellings): for example, coin/join/coil, tear/year/hear/near.

A Lesson for Every Day
Literacy
4–5 Years
© A&C Black

Match-up: 3

• **Join the** words **to the pictures.**

ladder

robber

dinner

hanger

powder

 **NOW TRY THIS!**

• **Read the words with a friend.**

quicker   lighter

Teachers' note Use this after teaching the /**er**/ phoneme, as in *boxer*. Ask the children to name and sound-talk the objects in the pictures. They can then join the words to the objects.

A Lesson for Every Day
Literacy
4–5 Years
© A&C Black

Sound change: 1

- **Read the** `word`.
- **Change the middle** `sound`.
- **Read the new word.**

Work in pairs.

ai

h	ee	l

→

h		l

igh

r	oo	t

→

oo

f	igh	t

→

ee

s	oo	n

→

NOW TRY THIS!

- **Make these into words.**

r		f	t	o	p

m		n	l		t

- **Say the words.**

Teachers' note Use this after the /ai/, /ee/, /oo/ and /igh/ phonemes have been learned. Model the first line: ask the children to read the word with a partner. Invite responses, and then point to the phoneme frame with the gap. Point out the letters **ai** above the arrow and ask the children to write them in the gap and then read the word with their partner.

A Lesson for Every Day
Literacy
4–5 Years
© A&C Black

Sound change: 2

- **Read the** `word` .
- **Change the middle** `sound` .
- **Read the new word.**

Work in pairs.

oo

b	oa	t

➔

b		t

or

f	ee	t

➔

f		t

ow

t	ur	n

➔

oi

c	oo	l

➔

NOW TRY THIS!

- **Make these into words.**

p	o	p	c		n

p		s	o	n

- **Say the words.**

Teachers' note Use this after the /oa/, /oo/, /ee/, /or/, /ur/, /ow/ and /oi/ phonemes have been learned. Model the first line: ask the children to read the word with a partner. Invite responses, and then point to the phoneme frame with the gap. Point out the letters **oo** above the arrow and ask the children to write them in the gap and then read the word with their partner.

A Lesson for Every Day
Literacy
4–5 Years
© A&C Black

Sound machines

- **Choose** sounds **from the sound machine.**
- **Write them in the gaps.**
- **Read the** words .

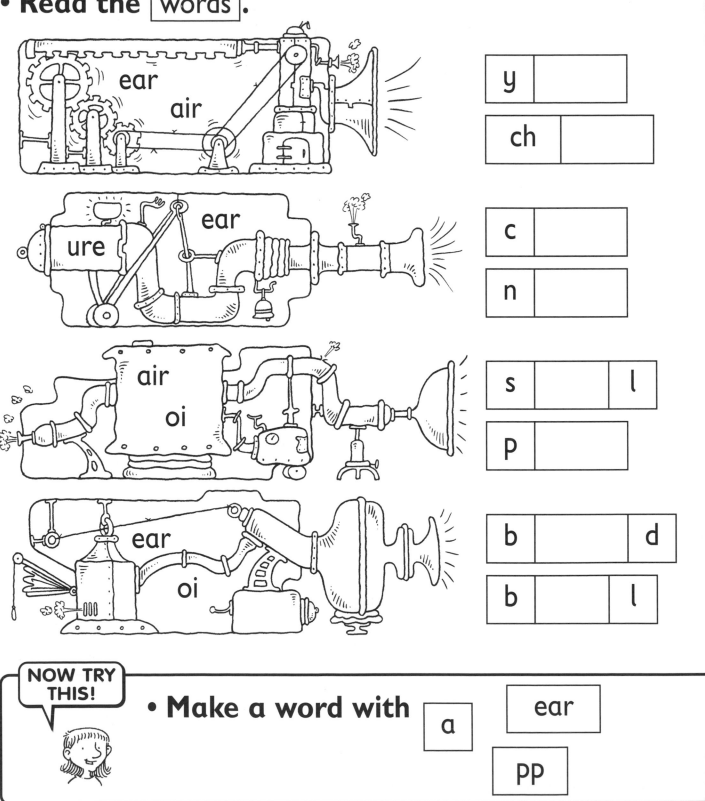

Teachers' note Use this after the /**air**/, /**ear**/, /**oi**/ and /**ure**/ phonemes have been learned. Model how to complete the activity using the first example: ask the children to sound the phonemes /**y**/ and /**ch**/ with /**ear**/ and /**air**/ and to decide which ones make real words. Some children might first need to try these out using magnetic letters or a wipe-off whiteboard.

A Lesson for Every Day
Literacy
4–5 Years
© A&C Black

Two letters – one sound: 1

Write ck in the gaps.
Say the sounds.
Say the word.

| d | u | |

| b | a | |

| s | i | |

| r | o | |

| s | a | |

| p | e | |

NOW TRY THIS!

• **Write two boys' names with** ck.
Begin with M **and** J.

Teachers' note Use this once the consonant phoneme /**ck**/ and 'two letters – one sound' have been taught. You could begin, orally, with everyday sounds represented by words containing **ck**: for example, *tick-tock* (and *clock*) and the nursery rhyme *Hickory, Dickory Dock*. The children could sound their completed words with a partner and then blend the phonemes to say the words.

A Lesson for Every Day
Literacy
4–5 Years
© A&C Black

129

Two letters – one sound: 2

- **Write** ss **or** zz **in the gaps.**
- **Say the** sounds .
- **Say the** word .

| f | i | |

| k | i | |

| h | i | |

| j | a | |

NOW TRY THIS!

- **Say the word.**
- **Write the word.**

Teachers' note This should be introduced once the children know the **ss** and **zz** graphemes representing the /**ss**/ and /**zz**/ phonemes respectively. By now they will be familiar with 'two letters – one sound'. Ask them what sound a bee makes. They could repeat *buzz*, emphasising the final /**z**/ sound – *buzzzzzzz*. Repeat for a snake – *hisssssss*.

130

A Lesson for Every Day
Literacy
4–5 Years
© A&C Black

Write th **in the gaps.**
Say the sounds .
Say the words .

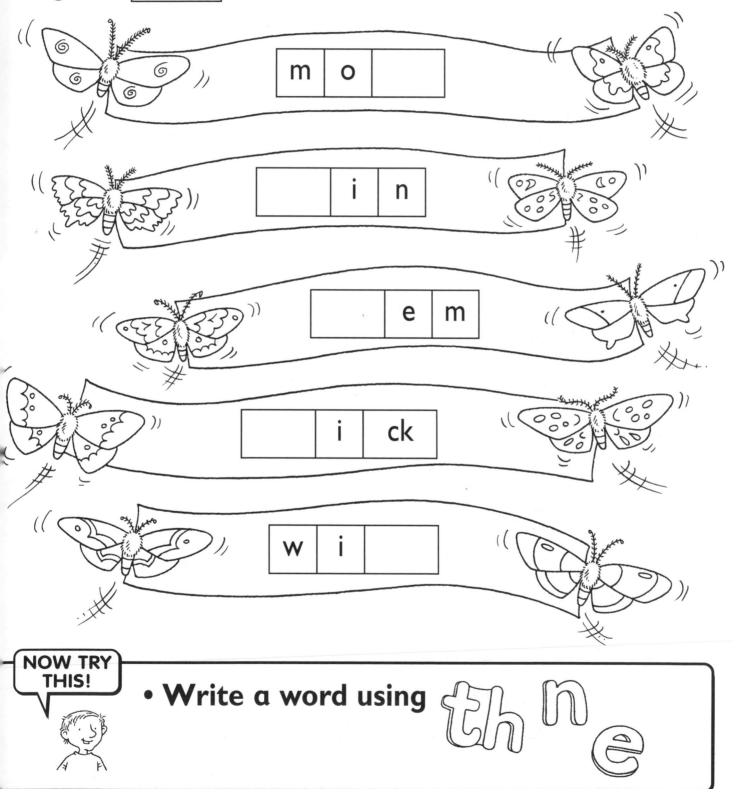

| m | o | |

| | i | n |

| | e | m |

| | i | ck |

| w | i | |

NOW TRY THIS!

• **Write a word using** th n e

Teachers' note This should be introduced once the children know the /th/ phoneme. By now they will be familiar with 'two letters – one sound'. Ask them if they know the name of the insect in the pictures. Tell them it is a moth and emphasise the final **th**; also remind them of the voiced /th/ phoneme in *the*. They could repeat the sentence *This is the moth* before they write the letters.

A Lesson for Every Day
Literacy
4–5 Years
© A&C Black

131

Partners: 1

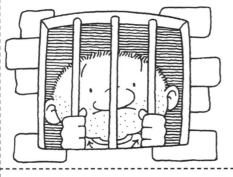
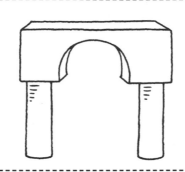

chain	sheep	teeth
jail	arch	cheek
farm	jacket	jeep

Teachers' note Use the cards for matching games. Mark or colour the backs of the cards to show whether they are word cards or picture cards. Place them face down. The children turn over one of each. If they match, they keep them; if not, they turn them face down, then it is the next child's turn. Continued on 'Partners: 2'.

A Lesson for Every Day
Literacy
4–5 Years
© A&C Black

Partners: 2

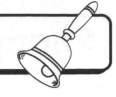

light	goat	moon
coach	torch	boot
cow	owl	quoit

Teachers' note Continued from 'Partners: 1'. An alternative game is to give each child a card (use as few or as many as you need), ensuring that for each picture card another child has the appropriate word card. Ask the children to find their partners.

A Lesson for Every Day
Literacy
4–5 Years
© A&C Black

133

Ready for action: words

sing a song	send a letter	float on my back
mix with a spoon	brush my hair	follow a snail trail
click my fingers	sleep in a tent at night	snap a twig
stack blocks	butter a cracker	brush my teeth

Teachers' note Use this with 'Ready for action: pictures'. Cut out the cards and give as many pairs of word and picture cards as appropriate to each pair of children. Let them read the words and match them to the pictures. These could also be used for matching games in which children have either a word or a picture card and have to find their partner.

A Lesson for Every Day
Literacy
4–5 Years
© A&C Black

Ready for action: pictures

Teachers' note Use this with 'Ready for action: words'. You could copy each page onto card of a different colour and place the cards face down in two sets. The children turn over a card from each set. If they match, they keep the pair; if not, they return the cards to their places, face down, then it is the next child's turn.

A Lesson for Every Day
Literacy
4–5 Years
© A&C Black

Question cards

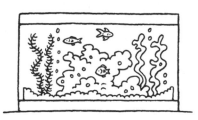

Is there pondweed
in the fish tank?

Can a rabbit
swim in the river?

Is the kitten
under the bed?

Did the pinch hurt?

Did the sun
melt the butter?

Do otters
have tusks?

Can you chop the
Moon with a spoon?

Can a cook
roast a parsnip?

Is there a shark
in the sandpit?

Will the jumper
have a soft landing?

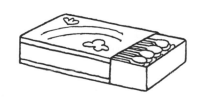

Is there milk
in the matchbox?

Is there a
light in the street?

Teachers' note Cut out the cards, which can be used in different ways. You could give each child a card and ask him or her to read the question aloud. The others have to answer yes or no; or let them do this in pairs, using several cards. Some children may need adult help with the reading of longer or unfamiliar words.

A Lesson for Every Day
Literacy
4–5 Years
© A&C Black

Titles

- **What are the stories about?**
- **Write** a boy , a girl , an animal **or** a food .

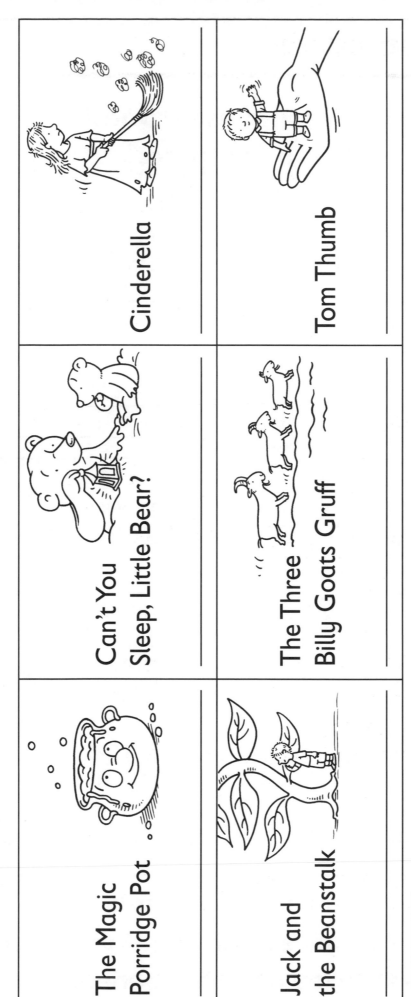

The Magic
Porridge Pot ....

Can't You
Sleep, Little Bear? ....

Cinderella ....

Jack and
the Beanstalk ....

The Three
Billy Goats Gruff ....

Tom Thumb ....

NOW TRY THIS!

- **Write what these books are about.**

Goldilocks and the Three Bears ....

Hansel and Gretel ....

Teachers' note Invite volunteers to identify each story and to say its title. Invite them to say whom the story is about and what happened. Read the words in the boxes with the children; ask them to decide what each story is about and to write it in the box.

A Lesson for Every Day
Literacy
4–5 Years
© A&C Black

137

Page match

- **What happened in these stories?**
- **Join the** `covers` **to the** `pages`.

The Very Hungry Caterpillar

Big Bear got a light for Little Bear.

Rosie's Walk

Chicken Licken

The caterpillar grew into a butterfly.

The Snowman

The hen went for a walk.

Can't You Sleep, Little Bear?

An acorn fell from the tree.

NOW TRY THIS!

- **Draw another book.**
- **Draw something that happened in it.**
- **Write what happened.**

Teachers' note Invite volunteers to identify each story and to say its title. Invite them to say who the first story is about and what happened in it. Model joining this 'cover' to the 'pages' that say what happened in the story. The children could then look at the other 'pages' and match these to the appropriate story. Children tackling the extension activity may need adult help with the writing.

A Lesson for Every Day
Literacy
4–5 Years
© A&C Black

Place to place

- **Read the words on the footprints.**
- **Write the sentences.**
- **Read the sentences.**

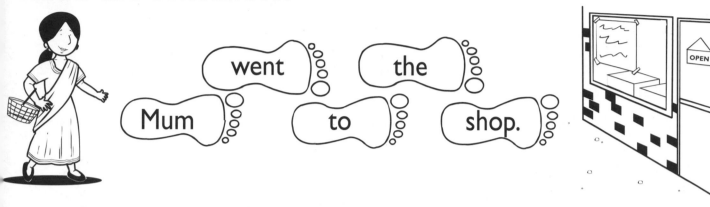

Mum went to the shop.

_____

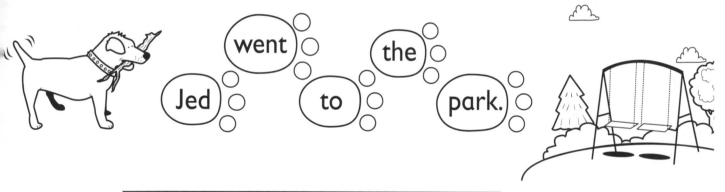

Jed went to the park.

_____

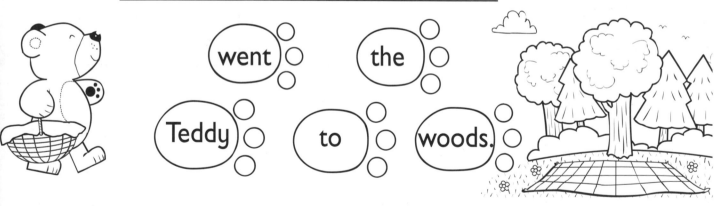

Teddy went to the woods.

_____

NOW TRY THIS!

- **Draw someone's footprints. Where did they go?**
- **Write a sentence.**

Use word-banks.

Teachers' note Ask the children to follow the footprints with a finger as you read the first sentence with them. Ask them to point to, and read, each word separately. Then ask them to reread the sentence. Draw out that the words make sense when they are put together like this; they make up a sentence. Also emphasise the direction of the order in which the words are read.

A Lesson for Every Day
Literacy
4–5 Years
© A&C Black

Name rhymes

- **Say the names of the children.**
- **Find the** | rhymes |.

Ann

Lee

Ben

sea

hen

fan

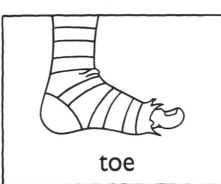
face

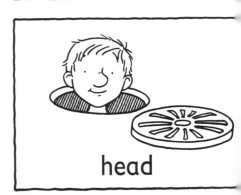
toe

head

Jo

Ed

Grace

NOW TRY THIS!

- **Draw things that rhyme with these.**

  Nell   Jane   Dat

- **Write the words.**

Teachers' note The children could first say the names of the children aloud and then repeat the circled name *Ben*. Point out the line joining the name to the picture and ask what this picture shows. What do they notice about the words *Ben* and *hen*? They can then join the other names to the pictures they rhyme with.

A Lesson for Every Day
Literacy
4–5 Years
© A&C Black

Same starters

The children do things that begin with the same sound as their names.

• **Write what they do.**

 James _____ sings

 Rani _____ hops

 William _____ jumps

 Sara _____ walks

 Harry _____ runs

NOW TRY THIS!

• **What do they do?**
• **Write the words.**

Peter _____ Ben _____

Dan _____ Lee _____

Teachers' note Bring out two of the children. Say their names, followed by an action beginning with the same sound: for example, *Robert reads, Sita sings*. Bring out two more children and invite the others to complete the sentences: for example, *Leo (laughs), Fay (falls, fights)*. Draw out that the actions begin with the same sounds as the names.

A Lesson for Every Day
Literacy
4–5 Years
© A&C Black

Acker Backer

- **Say the** rhyme **with a friend.**

Acker Backer

Soda cracker

Acker Backer four

Acker Backer

Soda cracker

Knock on Acker's door

NOW TRY THIS!

- **Say the rhyme again.**
- **Make up different claps.**

Teachers' note The children need plenty of space for this activity. Ask them to stand in pairs and to join in as you demonstrate this action rhyme with another adult. Make the hand clapping and thigh slapping fun. Point out that the children should only touch their partners' hands for the clapping – the other slapping actions are to do individually.

A Lesson for Every Day
Literacy
4–5 Years
© A&C Black

Dip, dip, dip

Say the [rhyme].
On each word, point to a sailor.
Which sailor do you finish on?

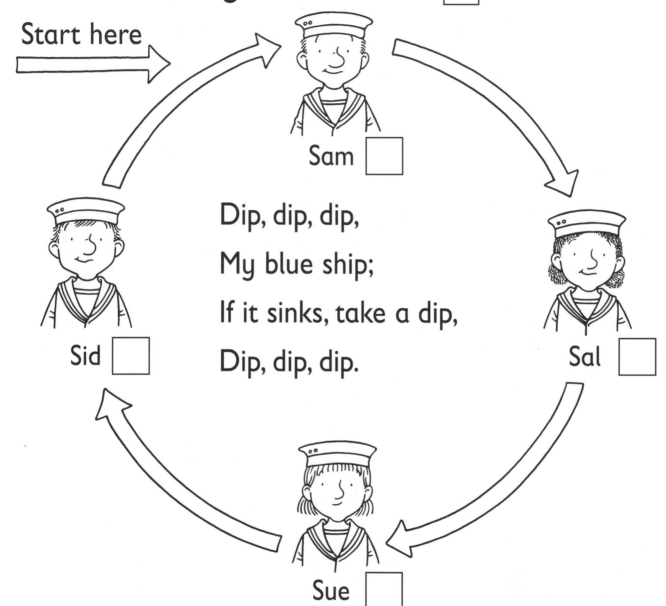

Start here

Sam ☐

Dip, dip, dip,

My blue ship;

If it sinks, take a dip,

Dip, dip, dip.

Sid ☐

Sal ☐

Sue ☐

NOW TRY THIS!

- **Say the rhyme again.**
- **Point to the sailors.**
- **Cross out the sailors you land on.**
- **Keep going until only one sailor is left.**

Teachers' note Using an enlarged copy of this page or a copy displayed on an interactive white-board, read the rhyme and demonstrate how to point to a sailor on each word, moving clockwise around the group. You could also ask the children to form a circle and have one stand in the centre and point to each child in turn, moving clockwise around the circle as they say the rhyme.

A Lesson for Every Day
Literacy
4–5 Years
© A&C Black

Character match: 1

Match the characters **from the same story.**

The Three Little Pigs

Gingerbread Man

The Three Bears

Red Riding Hood

Aladdin

Pinocchio

Rapunzel

Beauty

Chicken Licken

Character match: 2

Match the | characters | **from the same story.**

The Wolf

The Old Woman

Goldilocks

The Wolf

The Genie

Geppetto

The Witch

The Beast

Henny Penny

Teachers' note See also 'Character match: 1'. Copy these two pages onto thin card or laminate the paper copies; one set of cards can be used by a group of children. The cards can be used in various ways (see the notes on the activity page 18) which require the children to recognise characters from the same story.

A Lesson for Every Day
Literacy
4–5 Years
© A&C Black

Story things match

• **Match these things with the story characters.**

a house made
of straw

an oven

three bowls
of porridge

a basket

a lamp

a piece of wood

a tower

a rose

an acorn

Lost characters

Which characters have got lost?
Colour them.
Join them to their stories.

Goldilocks and the Three Bears

Jack and the Beanstalk

Little Red Riding Hood

The Three Billy Goats Gruff

NOW TRY THIS!

- Draw a picture of a story.
- Put a wrong character in it.
- Tell the new story to a friend.

Teachers' note Invite volunteers to identify each story and to say its title. Ask whom the first story is about and which characters in the picture do not belong there. They should colour these characters and then draw a line to join the characters to their own story.

A Lesson for Every Day
Literacy
4–5 Years
© A&C Black

147

The wrong order

- **Cut out the pages.**
- **Put them in order.**
- **Tell the** story **to a friend.**

Snap! A fox ate
the gingerbread man!

The gingerbread
man ran away.

An old woman
made a gingerbread man.

The old woman
chased after him.

NOW TRY THIS!

- **Draw four pictures of another story.**
- **Tell the story to a friend.**

Teachers' note *The children first need to have read* The Gingerbread Man. *Invite volunteers to say whom the story is about and what happened. Ask them to look at the pictures and to say what is happening in them. Read the captions with them. To order the pictures, the children could start by looking for the first and last parts, then the middle events.*

A Lesson for Every Day
Literacy
4–5 Years
© A&C Black

Story route cards

- **Tell one of the stories to a friend.**

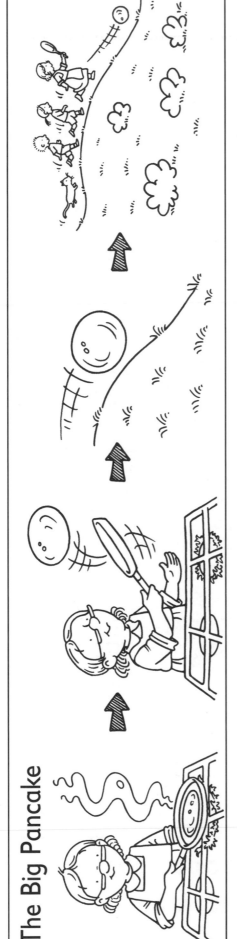

The Big Pancake

The Great Big
Enormous Turnip

seeds

- **Draw pictures to tell the rest of one of the stories.**

NOW TRY
THIS!

Teachers' note The children could use the route cards as prompts to help them to retell the stories but you could also use the cards to introduce the stories – as an 'appetiser' ask the children what the characters did and what happened to them. They can then find out, from the storybooks themselves, what happened next.

A Lesson for Every Day
Literacy
4–5 Years
© A&C Black

Information books

- **Choose a book for each child.**
- **Write his or her name under it.**

I like cars.

Jen

I like trees.

Raj

I like dogs.

Jim

I like birds.

Rob

I like football.

Sal

I like the moon.

Lee

Football

Cars

Dogs

Trees

Birds

The Moon

NOW TRY THIS!

- **Find a book about fish.**
- **Draw the cover.**

Teachers' note Ask volunteers to read what each person wants to find out about. Then read the titles of the books with the children. Show them how to write the person's name on the line below the book. Draw out that the titles of information books tell us what they are about.

150

A Lesson for Every Day
Literacy
4-5 Years
© A&C Black

Baby animals

sheep   lamb

cow   calf

pig   piglet

horse   foal

- **Write the** | missing words | .

A baby horse is a _____.   A baby sheep is a _____.

A baby cow is a _____.   A baby pig is a _____.

NOW TRY THIS!

- **Find out what their babies are called:**

cat   dog   hen

Use information books.

- **Write** | sentences | **about them.**

Teachers' note Ask the children to name the animals in the pictures and help them to read the captions. Tell them that these are pictures of the pages in books about animals. Point out that one animal on each page is the adult and the other is the baby. Ask them what the first missing word is and how they knew. Draw out that they found this out by looking at 'pages' from an information book.

A Lesson for Every Day
Literacy
4–5 Years
© A&C Black

Animal families

- **Read the words.**
- **Draw the animal.**
- **Write what it is.**

My baby is a calf.

My baby is a piglet.

My baby is a foal.

My baby is a lamb.

NOW TRY THIS!

- **Draw another animal talking about its baby.**
- **Ask a friend what it is.**

Teachers' note The children should first have completed 'Baby animals'. Invite a volunteer to read what the first animal is saying. Ask them to look at their completed copies of 'Baby animals'. Which animal's baby is a calf? Point out that they found this on an 'information book page' and that we use information books to find the answers to questions.

A Lesson for Every Day
Literacy
4–5 Years
© A&C Black

Animal homes

under the ground

in a pond

in the sea

in trees

Fill in the missing words **.**

An owl lives _____.

A frog lives _____.

A jellyfish lives _____.

A mole lives _____.

NOW TRY THIS!

• **Draw another animal in each animal home.**

Use information books.

Teachers' note Ask the children to name the animals in the pictures and to say where they live. Point out the text which tells us. Tell them that these are pictures of pages in a book about animals. Then read the first information sentence with them. Ask them what the missing words are and how they knew. Draw out that they found this out by looking at an information book.

A Lesson for Every Day
Literacy
4–5 Years
© A&C Black

Plants

- **Read about the plants.**
- **Colour them.**

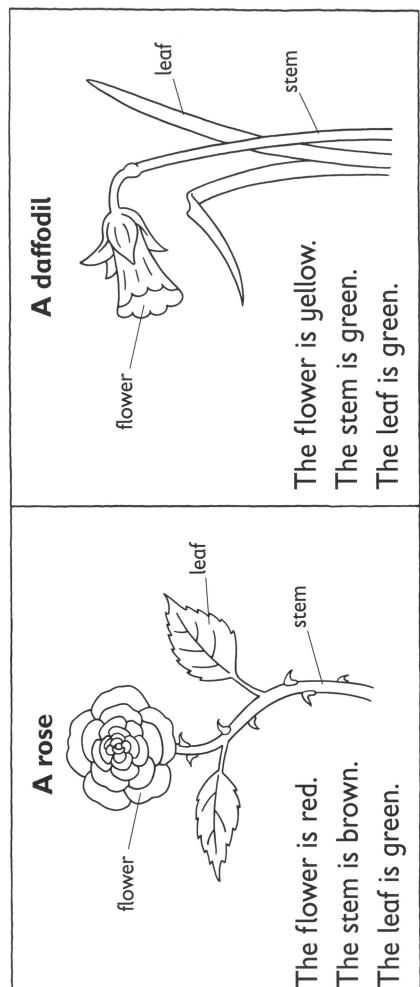

A daffodil

leaf

stem

flower

The flower is yellow.
The stem is green.
The leaf is green.

A rose

leaf

stem

flower

The flower is red.
The stem is brown.
The leaf is green.

A Lesson for Every Day
Literacy
4–5 Years
© A&C Black

Use information books.

NOW TRY THIS!

- **Draw another plant.**
- **Write a** sentence **about it.**

Teachers' note Ask the children to name the plants in the pictures and help them to read the labels.
Tell them that these are pictures of pages in an information book about plants. Then read the first
information sentence with them. Ask them what colour the flower is and how they know. Draw out that
they found this out by reading part of an information book.

How to make chocolate crispies

• **Put the pictures in** order .

How to make chocolate crispies

Mix the melted chocolate and cornflakes together.

Put a cherry on top.

Put the mixture into a cake case.

Melt the chocolate.

NOW TRY THIS!

• **What will you do next?**
• **Draw the next picture.**
• **Write about what it shows.**

Teachers' note Use a correctly ordered copy of this page to show the children how to make chocolate crispies. They should give the adult instructions for melting the chocolate. They could then follow the rest of the instructions. Afterwards, give them a set of pictures to put in order. Then ask them to read the instructions. Do they sound right? Finally, they could number the 'pages'.

A Lesson for Every Day
Literacy
4–5 Years
© A&C Black

Now and then

- **Look at the old objects.**
- **What do we use now?** ☑

> Use books and the Internet.

Old objects	What we use now
(kettle)	(mug) ☐ (iron) ☐ (electric kettle) ☐
(flat iron)	(ironing board) ☐ (dustpan and brush) ☐ (iron) ☐
(stove and stool)	(vacuum cleaner) ☐ (washing machine) ☐ (electric kettle) ☐
(gramophone)	(television) ☐ (mp3 player) ☐ (washing machine) ☐

NOW TRY THIS!

- **Find out what people used to use for:**

 lights   cookers

 156

Teachers' note Use this to introduce artefacts from the past. Give the children an opportunity to examine the objects or to look at pictures of them in an information book or on the Internet. Ask them what they think each one was for. Encourage them to compare them with things at home. They can then tick the box for the modern item that serves the same purpose.

A Lesson for Every Day
Literacy
4–5 Years
© A&C Black

Party time

To Het

Please come to my party

on Monday

at 4 o'clock

at 3 Top Lane

from Tom

• **Tick the correct answers.** ✔

• **When is the party?**

6 o'clock ☐

4 o'clock ☐

1 o'clock ☐

Monday ☐

Friday ☐

Sunday ☐

• **Where is the party?**

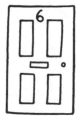 ☐

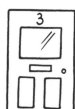 ☐

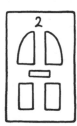 ☐

NOW TRY THIS!

• **Write Het's reply to Tom.**

Teachers' note Invite volunteers to read aloud the party invitation. Ask them if they have had party invitations. What does the invitation need to tell them? Read the first question and ask the children how they can find the answer. Point out that the invitation tells them. Discuss how to reply to a party invitation before the children tackle the extension activity.

A Lesson for Every Day
Literacy
4–5 Years
© A&C Black

The Three Little Pigs puppets

• **Use the finger puppets to tell the** story .

• **Draw a picture of one part of the story.**
• **Write a** caption .

Teachers' note Copy the page onto thin card. The children will need help in cutting out the finger holes. They first need to have read or listened to *The Three Little Pigs*. Ask them what the Three Little Pigs did. Ask them what the Wolf did and what he said. What did the Little Pigs say to him? The children could retell the story with a partner or group (see Notes on the activities, page 19).

A Lesson for Every Day
Literacy
4–5 Years
© A&C Black

Goldilocks puppets

• **Use the finger puppets to tell the** story .

NOW TRY THIS!

• **Draw something Goldilocks did.**
• **Write a** caption .

Teachers' note Copy the page onto thin card. The children will need help in cutting out the finger
oles. They first need to have read or listened to *Goldilocks and the Three Bears*. Ask them what
oldilocks did. Whose house did she go into? What did they say when they got back? The children
ould retell the story with a partner or group (see Notes on the activities, page 19).

A Lesson for Every Day
Literacy
4–5 Years
© A&C Black

159

Little Red Hen mask

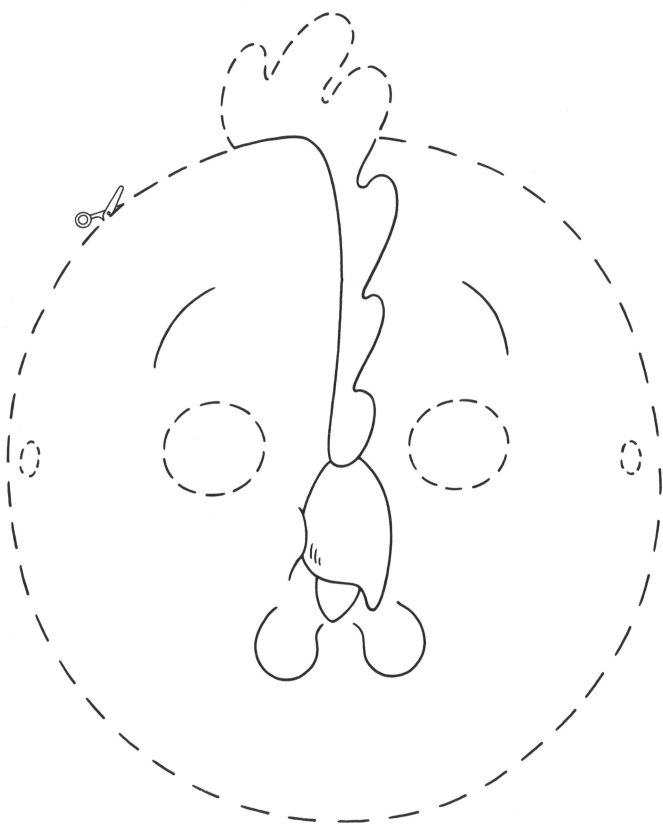

Teachers' note Copy the page onto thin card. Use this with 'Cat mask', 'Rat mask', 'Pig mask' and 'The little red hen'. The children first need to have read or listened to *The Little Red Hen*. Encourage them to join in the repeated words of the characters ('Who will help me…?' and 'Not I'). The masks can be used by a group of four children. Ask the child who is going to be the Little Red Hen what he or she will say.

A Lesson for Every Day
Literacy
4–5 Years
© A&C Black

Cat mask

A Lesson for Every Day
Literacy
4–5 Years
© A&C Black

161

Teachers' note Copy the page onto thin card. Use this with 'Little Red Hen mask', 'Rat mask', 'Pig mask' and 'The Little Red Hen'. The children first need to have read or listened to *The Little Red Hen*. Encourage them to join in the repeated words of the characters ('Who will help me…?' and 'Not I'). The masks can be used by a group of four children. Ask the child who is going to be the Cat what he or she will say.

Rat mask

Teachers' note Copy the page onto thin card. Use this with 'Little Red Hen mask', 'Cat mask', 'Pig mask' and 'The Little Red Hen'.. The children first need to have read or listened to *The Little Red Hen*. Encourage them to join in the repeated words of the characters ('Who will help me…?' and 'Not I'). The masks can be used by a group of four children. Ask the child who is going to be the Rat what he or she will say.

A Lesson for Every Day
Literacy
4–5 Years
© A&C Black

Pig mask

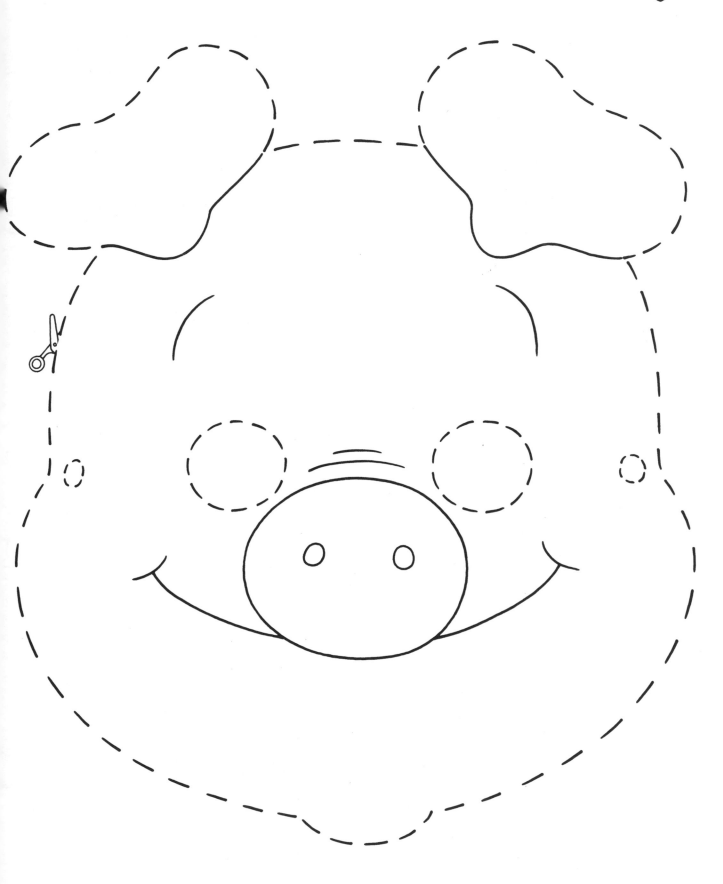

eachers' note Copy the page onto thin card. Use this with 'Little Red Hen mask', 'Cat mask', 'Rat ask' and 'The Little Red Hen'. The children first need to have read or listened to *The Little Red Hen*. ncourage them to join in the repeated words of the characters ('Who will help me...?' and 'Not I'). The asks can be used by a group of four children. Ask the child who is going to be the Pig what he or she ill say.

The Little Red Hen

- **Act the** story **with three friends.**

Who will help me to plant this wheat?

Not I. Not I. Not I.

Then I shall plant it myself.

Who will help me to cut the wheat?

Not I. Not I. Not I.

Then I shall cut it myself.

NOW TRY THIS!

- **What happens next?**
- **Act the rest of the story.**

 164 **Teachers' note** Copy the page onto thin card. Use this with 'Little Red Hen mask', 'Cat mask', 'Rat mask' and 'Pig mask'. The children first need to have read or listened to *The Little Red Hen*. They can use this page to help them to enact the story. Help them to read the repeated words of each character before they enact the story.

A Lesson for Every Day
Literacy
4–5 Years
© A&C Black

Picture story

Write the |words| **for the pictures.**
Read the |story|.

We went to the | f | | | f | | |.

We had some | c | | | | | s |

and some | p | | | c | | |.

There were | s | | | | s |

and a | h | | | | | | | | - | s | | | | | | |.

NOW TRY THIS!

• **Write another** |sentence| **for the story.**

Teachers' note The children could read the words with a partner and then decide what the pictures show. Ask them to sound-talk each word and then write it in the phoneme frame: *funfair, crisps, pop-corn, swings, helter-skelter*. Some children may need adult help as they sound-talk the longer words on this page.

A Lesson for Every Day
Literacy
4–5 Years
© A&C Black

That's wrong!

Teddy has made some mistakes.

- **Read the** sentences **and help Teddy to put them right.**

I can stir cream with a flag.

I can stir cream with

a ☐☐☐☐ .

Manesh has seven sticks

Manesh has ☐☐

☐☐☐☐☐ .

I push the car.

I ☐☐☐

the ☐☐☐☐ .

The crab is in the pool.

The ☐ s ☐☐☐☐

is on the ☐ r ☐☐ .

NOW TRY THIS!

- **Write a sentence about a park.**

Teachers' note Tell the children that Teddy has made one or two mistakes with each sentence. They have to find the mistakes and then write the correct words. Let them read the sentences aloud with a friend and write the correct words on the phoneme frames (or you could delete these and replace them with lines).

A Lesson for Every Day
Literacy
4–5 Years
© A&C Black

The party

Act the story with a friend.
Draw what happens next.
Write the words.

Is it time for the party?

No. It's time to get up.

Is it time for the party?

No. It's time for breakfast.

NOW TRY THIS!

- **Finish telling the story.**
- **Act it with a friend.**

Teachers' note Talk about events the children look forward to and how it feels to be waiting for an event. Read the question and answer in each picture, then invite the children to supply a question and answer for the third picture: for example, it might be time for school, lunch or shopping. Encourage them to draw hands on the clock to show the time.

A Lesson for Every Day
Literacy
4–5 Years
© A&C Black

167

Map: 1

- **Read the** ⬚speech bubbles⬚ **.**
- **Look at the map on sheet 2.**
- **Who lives in each house? Write the children's names by the houses.**

My house is by a big tree.

Ben

My house is number 2.

Ella

My house is by a pond.

Lee

My house is number 4.

Salim

My house is by a bridge.

Mari

My house is number 6.

May

NOW TRY THIS!

- **Draw a map of a road.**
- **Write names by the houses.**

Teachers' note Give each child a copy of this page and the map on 'Map: 2'. Read aloud the words in the first speech bubble, then invite the children to read the second and subsequent ones. Return to the first one and ask the children how they can find Sam's house on the map. They should write his name in the box and continue with the others.

A Lesson for Every Day
Literacy
4–5 Years
© A&C Black

Map: 2

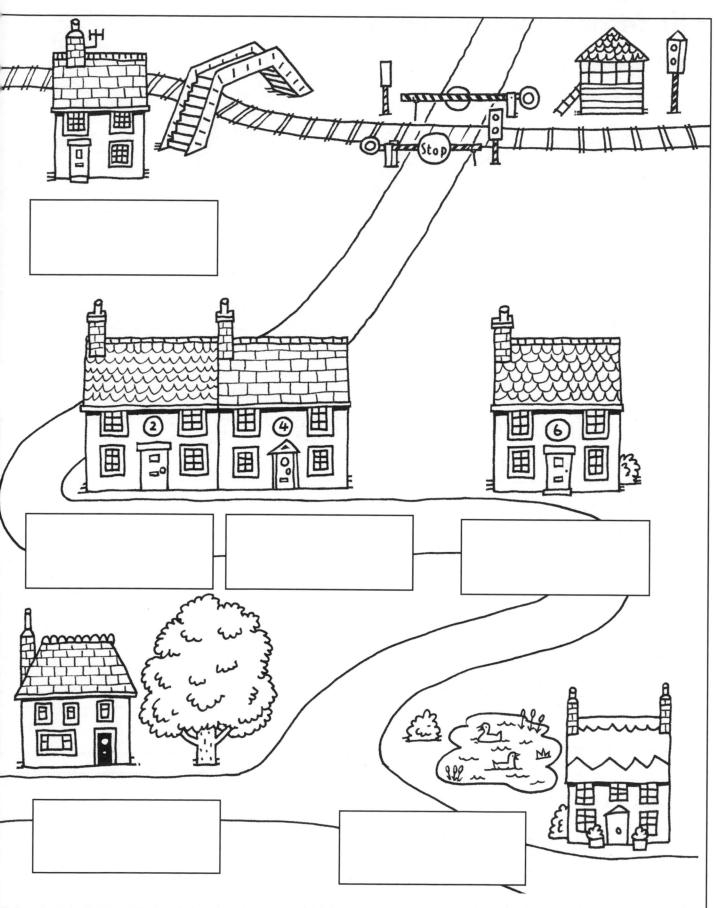

Teachers' note Use this with the activity on 'Map: 1'. When the children have completed the activity, they could use these characters and the setting as inspiration for a story.

A Lesson for Every Day
Literacy
4–5 Years
© A&C Black

The take-away

The family choose meals.

Dad goes to the take-away.

- **Write Dad's** [list] .

vegetable pizza

Dan — mushroom pizza

Alex — chicken and chips

Poppy

Mum — prawns with rice

Dad — burger and salad

NOW TRY THIS!

- **Work in a group.**
- **Each choose a meal.**
- **Write a list.**

Teachers' note Ask the children if their families sometimes have a take-away meal. Who goes to the shop? How does he or she remember what to buy? Draw out the need for a list. Help the children to read the thought bubbles. For the extension activity the children should work in small groups, each writing an individual list.

A Lesson for Every Day
Literacy
4–5 Years
© A&C Black

Wag goes shopping

Wag lives in a little house by the sea.
One day Wag goes shopping.

• Write Wag's |list|.

bone   meat   dish

biscuits   ball   shampoo

Shopping list

_____

_____

_____

_____

_____

_____

NOW TRY THIS!

A cat named Purr lives by Wag.
• **Write Purr's shopping list.**

Teachers' note Begin by asking the children about shopping trips with their family. How does their mother, father or other adult remember what to buy? Draw out the need for a list. Help the children to read Wag's thought bubble. For the extension activity, ask the children to think about what a cat needs. Might Purr buy any of the same things as Wag?

Misa's sleepover

What is Misa packing?
- **Write her** ⬚list⬚.

hairbrush

slippers

pyjamas

toothbrush

book

teddy

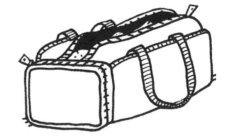

Misa's sleepover list

_____

_____

_____

_____

_____

_____

NOW TRY THIS!

What would you pack for a holiday at the seaside?
- **Write a list.**

Teachers' note Show the children the picture and talk about what Misa is doing. Ask how she will remember to pack everything and how she can make sure that it all goes back in her bag when she comes home. Draw out the need for a list. As a follow-up activity, the children could draw and write their own sleepover packing lists.

A Lesson for Every Day
Literacy
4–5 Years
© A&C Black

At the zoo: 1

What is at the zoo?
- Cut along the dashes.
  Fold the flaps up.
  Write on the signs .

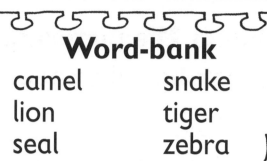

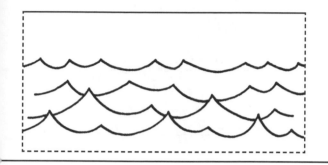

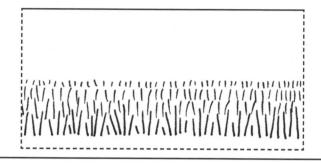

eachers' note Use this with 'At the zoo: 2'. When photocopying these pages, take care to make ccurate photocopies (or you can print out the pages from the CD-ROM). The children should first olour the pictures. Then help them to cut along the dotted lines by cutting in from the edge of the age. They should then carefully fold each flap along the unbroken line.

A Lesson for Every Day
Literacy
4-5 Years
© A&C Black

173

- **Colour the pictures.**
- **Carefully glue sheet 1 on top of this one.**

Teachers' note Continued from 'At the zoo: 1'. Tell the children to turn the first sheet face down and spread glue on the top and bottom edges, then to line it up carefully on top of this page and press down. The flaps can then be lifted to reveal the pictures. Ask the children how signs are helpful in a zoo, and who reads them. Encourage them to write signs for the animals hidden under the flaps.

A Lesson for Every Day
Literacy
4–5 Years
© A&C Black

Doors

How do these doors open?
Write signs on the doors.

Word-bank
lift   pull   push   turn

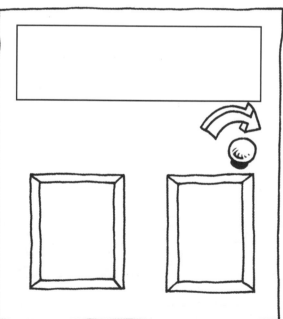

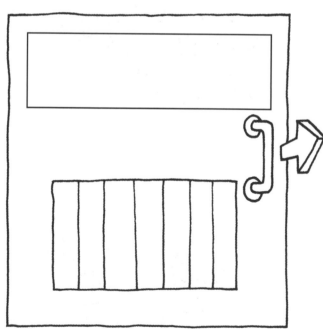

NOW TRY THIS!

• Write signs for doors at your school.

Teachers' note Begin by taking the children to look at signs on or near doors around the school. Read them with the children and discuss how they are useful. Ask what might happen if there were no signs on the doors. Look at the different kinds of door illustrated on the activity sheet and talk about how to open each one and what the sign should say.

A Lesson for Every Day
Literacy
4–5 Years
© A&C Black

My week: 1

- ## Draw and write what you did each day.

On Monday _____

_____

_____

On Tuesday _____

_____

_____

On Wednesday _____

_____

_____

On Thursday _____

_____

_____

Teachers' note Show the children some diaries and discuss how people use them. Focus on the use of a diary to record what has happened. The children could write their diary entry on the activity sheet at the end of each day, choosing one event to draw and write about. Provide fine felt-tipped pens or crayons for drawing small pictures. Continued on 'My week: 2'.

A Lesson for Every Day
Literacy
4–5 Years
© A&C Black

My week: 2

Write what you did each day.

On Friday _____

_____

_____

On Saturday _____

_____

_____

On Sunday _____

_____

_____

NOW TRY THIS!

• **Choose a story character.**
• **Write a** diary **for him or her.**

eachers' note Continued from 'My week: 1'. To help the children write their diary entries for
aturday and Sunday, ask them on Monday to talk about what they did on Saturday and Sunday
ntroducing the term *weekend*). For the extension activity, explain that they should imagine they are a
haracter from a well-known story and write sentences using 'I'.

A Lesson for Every Day
Literacy
4–5 Years
© A&C Black

Cinderella's shopping list

What does Cinderella need?

- **Write four things on the shopping list.**

Shopping list

one _____

one _____

six _____

six _____

Word-bank

lizards   pumpkin

mice   rat

NOW TRY THIS!

- **Write a shopping list for another story character.**

Use word-banks.

Teachers' note Reread the part of *Cinderella* where the fairy godmother sends Cinderella to find objects she can turn into a coach, horses, driver and footmen. Discuss how Cinderella will remember what she has to find, and introduce the idea of a shopping list. Help the children to read the words in the word-bank. They should then be able to complete the list.

A Lesson for Every Day
Literacy
4–5 Years
© A&C Black

My day

List the things you will do today.

Date: _____

Morning

_____

_____

_____

_____

_____

Afternoon

_____

_____

_____

_____

_____

NOW TRY THIS!

- **Write a 'things to do' list for a story character.**

Use a word-bank.

eachers' note Remind the children that people write lists to help them to remember things. Discuss
e different things the children do each day, and ask them how they remember to do them. Draw
tention to any lists used in the classroom. This list format can be used to help the children to list daily
sks. They could use word-banks to help them to complete it.

A Lesson for Every Day
Literacy
4-5 Years
© A&C Black

Teddy bears' picnic

- ## Choose the picnic menu for today.
- ## Write the menu.

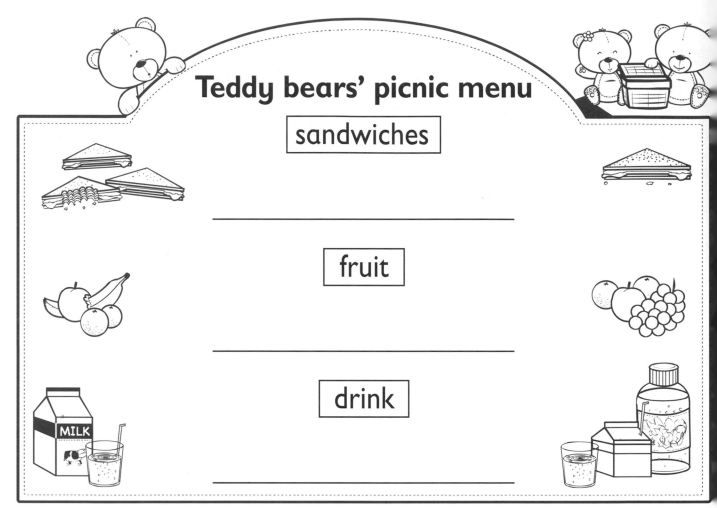

Teddy bears' picnic menu

sandwiches

_____

fruit

_____

drink

_____

Word-bank apple   egg   orange
banana   juice   tuna
cheese   milk   water

NOW TRY THIS!

- ## Draw and write a picnic menu for you.

Teachers' note It is useful if the children have first sung the song *Teddy Bears' Picnic*. Also show them some simple menus, preferably illustrated, and discuss what a menu is for. Help them to read the words in the word-bank and ask them to choose some foods for the teddy bears.

A Lesson for Every Day
Literacy
4–5 Years
© A&C Black

Little Red Riding Hood's basket

What is in Little Red Riding Hood's basket?

Write a list.

Little Red Riding
Hood's basket

_____

_____

_____

_____

_____

Grandma's House

flowers

cat

bread

book

grapes

NOW TRY THIS!

What would you take for Grandma?

- ## Write a list.
- ## Draw your basket.

Teachers' note The children should first have read or listened to the story of _Little Red Riding Hood_. Remind them of their previous learning about shopping lists before they look at Little Red Riding Hood's basket and take turns to identify something in it. They can then list these on the shopping list. Emphasise that they have written _words_.

A Lesson for Every Day
Literacy
4–5 Years
© A&C Black

This way

- ## Write the words on the signs.

beach

park

shops

woods

- ## Write a sign for a place you know.

Teachers' note Remind the children of the signs they wrote for the animals in *Pets' corner* and discuss other uses of signs: for example, to tell people the way to places. Ask the children to read the words in the word-bank and ask them to match them to the pictures beside the signs. Emphasise that these are *words*. They should then be able to copy the correct word onto each sign.

182

A Lesson for Every Day
Literacy
4–5 Years
© A&C Black

Teddy's party

t is Teddy's birthday.

He is having a party.

Make an invitation.

Please come to
my party on

_____ day

_____

at _____ o'clock

in Class _____ .

NOW TRY THIS!

- **Cut out the card.**
- **On the back write**
  To _____ **and** From _____

Teachers' note Provide a collection of printed party invitations for the children to read. What are invitations for? Ask the children what they need to tell the person (see Introduction). You could decide, as
a group or class, on what day the party is to be, where and at what time. Each member of the group
could send an invitation to someone at school.

A Lesson for Every Day
Literacy
4–5 Years
© A&C Black

Dear Humpty Dumpty

- **Write a letter to Humpty Dumpty.**
- **Tell him how to stay safe.**

Dear _____

_____

_____

_____

_____

From _____

Word-bank

and	fall	not	sit
can	get	off	wall
do	hurt	safe	you

NOW TRY THIS!

- **Make an envelope for your letter.**
- **Write Humpty Dumpty on it.**

Teachers' note The children first need to have heard and recited the nursery rhyme *Humpty Dumpty*. Ask them what they would like to write to Humpty Dumpty and encourage them to use the word-bank to write sentences. They should read their sentences aloud to check that they make sense.

A Lesson for Every Day
Literacy
4–5 Years
© A&C Black

Crazy cloakroom

• **Help the children to find their coats and bags.**

Tom	May	Ben	Bav	Zul	Ann

Zul Ann Tom

May Ben Bav

NOW TRY THIS!

• **Write your name on the label.**

eachers' note Ask the children to look for a name label in their coat or other garment. They could
ead one another's name labels and then hang them in the correct places by matching the name
abels. Ask them what the picture shows and how the children can find their coats. Point out how the
xample has been completed and ask them to draw lines to join the children to their coats.

A Lesson for Every Day
Literacy
4–5 Years
© A&C Black

My book

- **Write the children's names on their bookplates.**

Ella

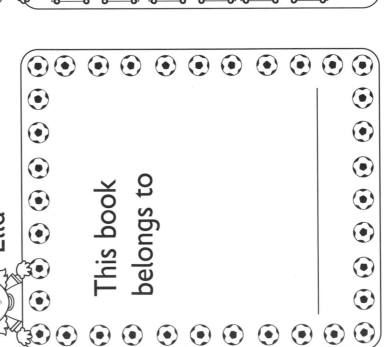

This book belongs to

Sam

This book belongs to

Amy

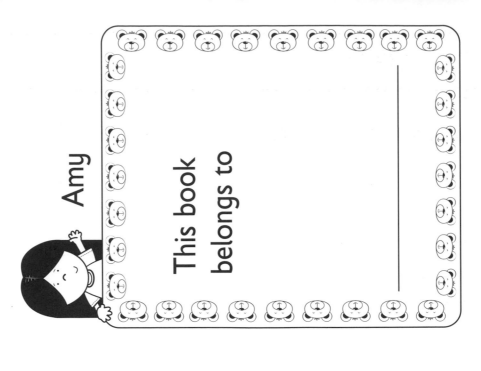

This book belongs to

- **Make a bookplate for a friend.**

NOW TRY THIS!

Teachers' note Show the children a book in which a bookplate has been fixed to show whom it belongs to. Read the bookplate with them, pointing to each word. Select individual words and ask, 'What does this word say?' Then tell the children that all the words together make up a sentence. They can then complete the bookplates. Ask them to read each sentence.

A Lesson for Every Day
Literacy
4–5 Years
© A&C Black

Pets' corner

Write the words on the signs.

Word-bank

cat

dog

fish

parrot

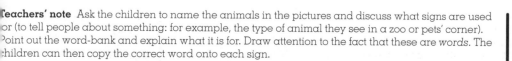

Teachers' note Ask the children to name the animals in the pictures and discuss what signs are used for (to tell people about something: for example, the type of animal they see in a zoo or pets' corner). Point out the word-bank and explain what it is for. Draw attention to the fact that these are *words*. The children can then copy the correct word onto each sign.

A Lesson for Every Day
Literacy
4–5 Years
© A&C Black

All wrong!

- **The signs are wrong.**
- **Cross out the wrong signs.**
- **Write the correct words.**

Word-bank

down

pull

push

up

NOW TRY THIS!

- **Make a sign to help visitors at your school.**

Use word-banks.

Teachers' note *Remind the children of the signs they wrote for the animals in* Pets' corner *and* This way *and discuss other uses of signs: for example, to help people to use things. Ask the children to read the words on the signs and to look at the pictures. Ask them what they* should *say. Can they find the correct* words *in the word-bank? They can then copy the correct word onto each sign.*

A Lesson for Every Day
Literacy
4–5 Years
© A&C Black

Names

- **Write the names.**
Begin with a capital letter.

Aa
Bb
Cc
Dd
Ee
Ff
Gg
Hh
Ii
Jj
Kk
Ll
Mm
Nn
Oo
Pp
Qq
Rr
Ss
Tt
Uu
Vv
Ww
Xx
Yy
Zz

andrew

carly

faria

harry

lee

tina

NOW TRY THIS!

- **Write the names of the people in your family.**

Teachers' note Point out that this page is about special words: the names of people. Explain that because they are special words they begin with a capital letter. The children could then look for the first
letter of their name and its corresponding lower-case letter in the alphabet chart above. Help them to
read the names and then ask them to copy them but begin with a capital letter.

A Lesson for Every Day
Literacy
4–5 Years
© A&C Black

Name that dog

- **Give the dogs names.**
- **Write on their bowls.**

Names start with a capital letter.

Aa
Bb
Cc
Dd
Ee
Ff
Gg
Hh
Ii
Jj
Kk
Ll
Mm
Nn
Oo
Pp
Qq
Rr
Ss
Tt
Uu
Vv
Ww
Xx
Yy
Zz

NOW TRY THIS!

- **Write the names of your friends' pets.**

Teachers' note It is useful if the children first complete 'Names'. Point out that this page, too, is about special words. They are special because they are the names of dogs. Discuss the names of dogs they know and help them to think up some others. Write these up in the form of a 'Dogs' name-bank' on the board or interactive whiteboard.

A Lesson for Every Day
Literacy
4–5 Years
© A&C Black

Capital I

You can use **I** instead of your name.
Write **I** in the gaps.
Read the sentences.

___ can't fly.

____ eat fruit.

___ am not a cat.

____ go to school.

___ am not a baby.

____ read books.

NOW TRY THIS!

• **Write two more sentences with I.**

eachers' note Bring a child out to the front and ask one of the others to say his or her name. Ask the
hers to make up a sentence about this child. Then ask the child to say it. Does it sound right? Draw
ut that he or she should say 'I' instead of his or her name. Point out that this is always a capital I.

A Lesson for Every Day
Literacy
4–5 Years
© A&C Black

I see

- **Write your name in the gaps.**
- **Read the sentences.**

_____ can sing.

_____ likes to play.

_____ sits here.

_____ is great!

- **Write the sentences again.**
- **Write** **I** **instead of your name.**
- **Read the sentences.**
- **Circle the other words you needed to change.**

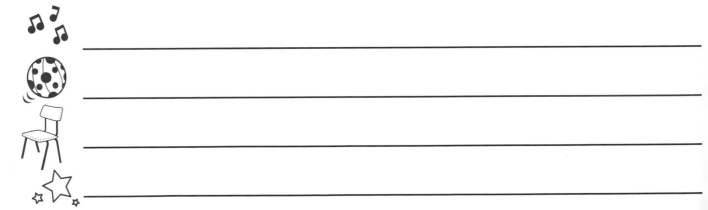

NOW TRY THIS!

- **Write two other sentences beginning with your own name.**
- **Write them again with** **I** **instead of your name.**

Teachers' note The children should first have completed 'Capital I'. Remind them of the sentences they made up about someone and how that person changed the name in the sentence to 'I'.

A Lesson for Every Day
Literacy
4–5 Years
© A&C Black

Starting off

Capital letters start a sentence.

S | <u>S</u>ix socks are in the box.

• Write the capital letter in the gap.

F | ___ive foxes ran away.

N | ___ine nets fell on the floor.

E | ___leven eggs broke.

O | ___ne old ox is eating grass.

 NOW TRY THIS!

• **Write sentences beginning with**

A and T

Teachers' note Make a simple sentence of words made up of plastic or wooden letters or written on the interactive whiteboard but with the first letter of the first word missing. What is wrong with this sentence? Add the missing letter and point out that a capital letter is needed to get a sentence started. Read the sentences on this page and ask what is wrong with them.

A Lesson for Every Day
Literacy
4–5 Years
© A&C Black

Start with a capital

Sentences start with a capital letter.
- **Circle the letter which should be a capital.**
- **Write each sentence correctly.**

(t)he old man had a red hat.

<u>The old man had a red hat.</u>

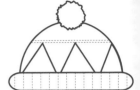

 it's time for tea.

_____

you did very well.

_____

 my cat is called Fluff.

_____

a rat hid under the box.

_____

 hens lay eggs.

_____

 194

Teachers' note The children should first have completed 'Starting off'. Read these sentences with them. This time there are no letters missing, but what is wrong with the sentences? The children can then rewrite the sentences but use a capital letter to begin the first word (referring to an alphabet chart if necessary).

A Lesson for Every Day
Literacy
4–5 Years
© A&C Black

A full stop

This is a full stop: ☐ .

It is a dot.

It goes at the end of a sentence.

- **Put a tick if the full stop is right.** ✓
- **Put a cross if it is wrong.** ☒

 Omar ate one orange˙ ☒

 Ted ate two toffees. ☐

 Theo ate three things. ☐

 Finn ate four fish fingers. ☐

 Fay ate five figs˙ ☐

 Selina ate six sausages: ☐

 Simon ate seven sultanas. ☐

 **NOW TRY THIS!**

- **Write two sentences about things you ate yesterday.**

 Remember the full stops.

Teachers' note Remind the children of their work on capital letters. Emphasise that a capital letter gets a sentence started. Point out that something is needed to stop it before the next sentence, and show them how to make a full stop. They could practise drawing full stops at the right size and on the line on which they write. They can then spot the correct and incorrect full stops.

A Lesson for Every Day
Literacy
4–5 Years
© A&C Black

Stop it!

A full stop ends a sentence.

Today we went to the zoo.

Stop.

• Put a full stop at the end of each sentence.

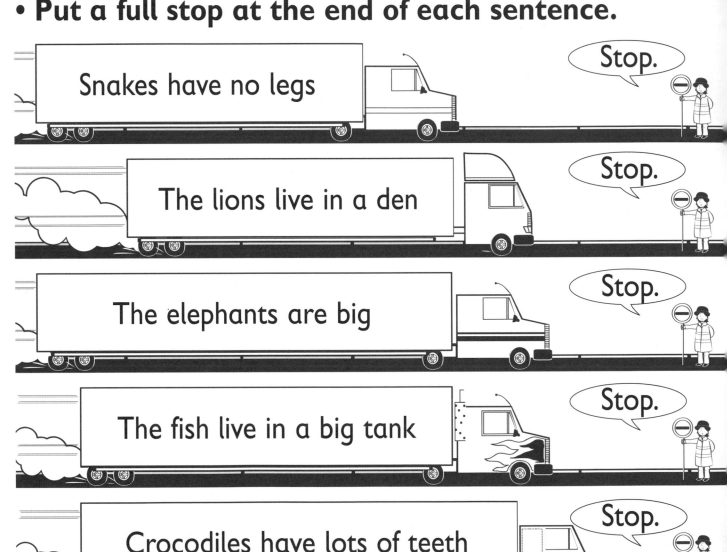

Snakes have no legs

Stop.

The lions live in a den

Stop.

The elephants are big

Stop.

The fish live in a big tank

Stop.

Crocodiles have lots of teeth

Stop.

NOW TRY THIS!

• **Write two other sentences about zoo animals.**

Remember the full stops.

Teachers' note The children should first have completed 'A full stop'. Remind them that a full stop ends a sentence and remind them of the size and position of a full stop. You could read these sentences one after the other without stopping, to demonstrate what happens if there are no full stops (you don't know where to stop). They can then add the full stops to these sentences.

A Lesson for Every Day
Literacy
4–5 Years
© A&C Black

Full stop finder: 1

Read the sentences.
Put in the full stops.

A sentence can go past the end of a line.

Today we are going to the park after school

Mum said that I can have some new shoes

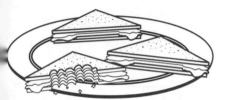

Lee and Raj came to my house for tea on Monday

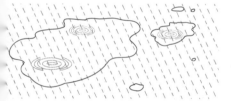

It rained all day so I couldn't play in the garden

I will be five years old on my birthday

Ask your dad if you can come to my party

NOW TRY THIS!

- **Circle the wrong full stops.**

I like. red jam. I don't like blue. jam. Dad likes green jam.

Teachers' note Begin by reading the first sentence aloud and asking the children to point out where it ends. If they point to the end of the line, read the sentence as if there were a full stop after 'park'. Ask the children if 'after school' makes sense as a sentence. Remind them that a sentence says what is happening.

A Lesson for Every Day
Literacy
4–5 Years
© A&C Black

Full stop finder: 2

Check for mistakes.

- **Put in the full stops.**
- **Read the sentences.**

We went to the shops We saw Jack and Lucy

I like fish and chips I don't like ham

A baby bear is called a cub A baby dog is a puppy

I saw Liz do a jig We saw Pip and Meg hop

NOW TRY THIS!

- **Put in the full stops.**
- **Read the sentences.**

The reds got a goal It was two goals to nil The reds will win the game

Teachers' note The children should first have completed 'Full stop finder: 1'. Read the first example aloud without stopping for breath between the two sentences. Ask the children if this sounds right. Help them to identify the end of the first sentence. If necessary, read other examples in this way to help the children to understand that a sentence does not always finish at the end of a line.

A Lesson for Every Day
Literacy
4–5 Years
© A&C Black

What did they do?

Write a word in each gap.

Choose words from the word-bank.

Word-bank

fell   sang

had   saw

ran

Raj _____ a cap.

May _____ fast.

I _____ a star.

Dad _____ down the steps.

Anna _____ a song.

NOW TRY THIS!

- **Write a sentence for each word.**

  like   have   go

eachers' note Read the first line of words with the children and ask them if it makes sense as a sentence. Ask them to choose a word from the word-bank to fill the gap. Draw out that the sentence now ays what is going on.

A Lesson for Every Day
Literacy
4–5 Years
© A&C Black

199

The big dog

- **Look at the pictures.**
- **Read the words.**
- **Join the bones to make sentences.**

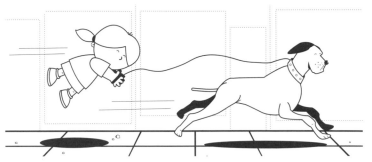

ran down the road

ate some meat

hid in a bin

played with a ball

The big dog played

in a bin.

The big dog hid

down the road.

The big dog ran

with a ball.

NOW TRY THIS!

What else did the big dog do?
- **Write a sentence.**

_____

Teachers' note Ask the children what the big dog did in each picture. Read the words with them. Ask them what the big dog played with and show them how to draw a line to join up the bones so that two sets of words make a sentence. You could use the terms 'beginning' and 'ending': 'What is the beginning of the sentence?', 'What is the ending of the sentence?'

A Lesson for Every Day
Literacy
4–5 Years
© A&C Black

Sentence factory

Choose a word from each box.
Write a sentence.
Read the sentence.

Does it make sense?

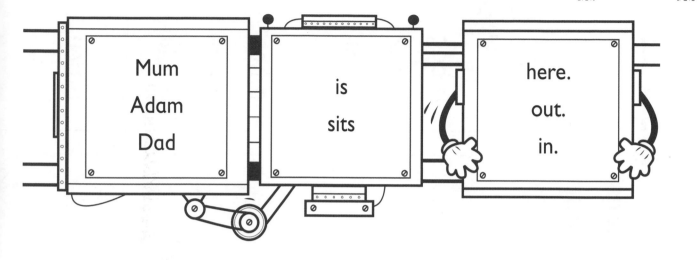

Mum		here.
Adam	is	out.
Dad	sits	in.

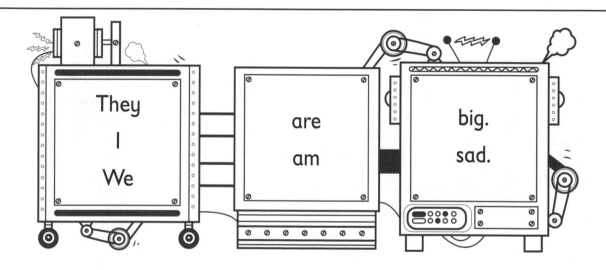

They		
I	are	big.
We	am	sad.

NOW TRY THIS!

- **Write another sentence with the words in the top machine.**
- **Write another sentence with the words in the bottom machine.**
Do your sentences make sense?

Teachers' note Help the children to make a sentence from the first 'machine' by choosing a word from each part of it. Ask them to write the sentence on the line below the machine. They can then do the same with the second machine and, in the extension activity, make a different sentence from the words in each machine.

A Lesson for Every Day
Literacy
4–5 Years
© A&C Black

Silly sentences

- Use the word-banks to make silly sentences.
- Write your sentences on a new piece of paper.

Word-bank

Curly

Ella

Grandad

Leo

Mum

Tibby

Word-bank

ate
bit
cooked
found
hid
hit
hugged
lost
made
painted

patted
saw

Word-bank

a bag
a cake
a doll
a fan
a hat
a jug
a lolly
a mop
a pen
a rat

a rock
a tree
a van
a yam

Teachers' note This is a game of 'consequences'. Ask the children to work in groups of three. Use the word-banks for reference and give each child a blank strip of paper. Each child writes a name from the first word-bank at the top of the strip, folds it under and passes it to the next player, who writes a word from the second column, etc. Once finished, the strips can be opened and the resulting sentences read aloud.

A Lesson for Every Day
Literacy
4–5 Years
© A&C Black

The park

Look at the picture.
What can you see?
Write the missing words.

can see a _____.

can see _____.

can _____.

_____.

NOW TRY THIS!

- **Draw a picture of your playground.**
- **Write a sentence about it.**

eachers' note Ask the children what the picture shows and what they can see in the park. Help them to complete the first sentence. They can then complete the sentences using this as a model and the abels to help them to spell the words. Draw out that they have written a caption which is a sentence.

A Lesson for Every Day
Literacy
4–5 Years
© A&C Black

203

Zoo time

What is at the zoo?
• Write the missing words.

At the zoo there is a _____

At the zoo there is _____

At the zoo there _____

At the zoo _____

At the _____

_____

NOW TRY THIS!

What else could there be at the zoo?
• Write two sentences.

204 Teachers' note Ask the children what the picture shows and what they can see in the zoo. Help them to complete the first sentence. They can then complete the sentences using this as a model and the labels to help them to spell the words. Draw out that they have written a caption which is a sentence.

A Lesson for Every Day
Literacy
4-5 Years
© A&C Black

In the street

What is there in the street?
Write the missing words.

bus stop

café

Cafe

Florist

shop

Open

bin

post box

crossing

kerb

There is a shop in the street.

There is a _____ in the street.

_____ in the street.

_____ .

_____ .

_____ .

_____ .

NOW TRY THIS!

• **Draw your street.**
• **Write two sentences about it.**

Teachers' note Ask the children what the picture shows and what they can see in the street. Help them to complete the first sentence. They can then complete the sentences using this as a model and the labels to help them to spell the words. Draw out that they have written a caption which is a sentence.

A Lesson for Every Day
Literacy
4–5 Years
© A&C Black

On the beach

- **What can you find on the beach?**
- **Write the missing words.**

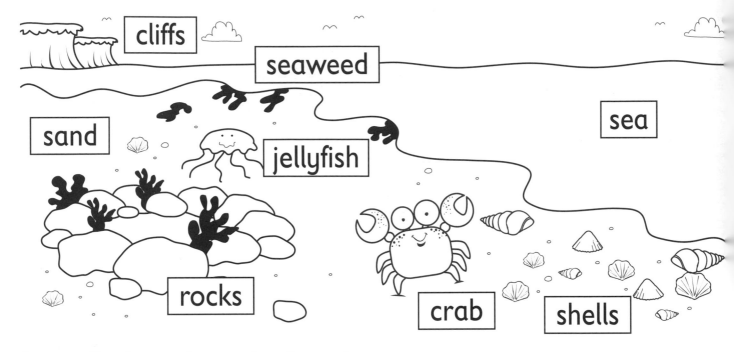

cliffs

seaweed

sea

sand

jellyfish

rocks

crab

shells

I can find sand on the beach.

I can find _____ on the beach.

I can find _____ on _____.

I can _____.

_____.

_____.

_____.

NOW TRY THIS!

What have you found on the beach?

- **Write two sentences.**

Teachers' note Ask the children what the picture shows and what they can see on the beach. Help them to complete the first sentence. They can then complete the sentences using this as a model and the labels to help them to spell the words. Draw out that they have written a caption which is a sentence.

A Lesson for Every Day
Literacy
4–5 Years
© A&C Black

Treasure hunt

Follow the treasure hunt.
Finish the sentences.

found a bag.

Then I found a _____.

Then I found a _____.

Then I found a _____.

Then I found a _____.

NOW TRY THIS!

- **Make a treasure hunt for a friend.**
- **Write what your friend finds.**

Teachers' note Help the children to follow the trail of the treasure hunt. Point out the first sentence and then continue along the trail, saying, 'Then I found a ...' (ask the children to supply the missing word). Continue to the end. Then let the children repeat this with a partner and write the sentences, using the first one as a model and the captions to help them to spell the words.

A Lesson for Every Day
Literacy
4–5 Years
© A&C Black

Look at the pictures of Sooty.

• **Finish the sentences.**

walks

sits

runs

jumps

eats

sleeps

Sooty walks.

Then Sooty _____.

Then Sooty _____.

Then _____.

Then _____.

_____.

NOW TRY THIS!

• **Play follow my leader with a friend.**
• **Draw what you do.**
• **Write sentences about it.**

Teachers' note Help the children to follow Sooty's walk, saying, 'Sooty walks.' Point out the first sentence and then continue, saying, 'Then Sooty …' (ask the children to supply the missing word). Continue to the last caption and then let the children repeat this with a partner and write the sentences, using the first one as a model and the captions to help them to spell the words.

A Lesson for Every Day
Literacy
4–5 Years
© A&C Black

Along the street: 1

- Four can play.
- Roll a dice.
- Move your counter.
- Pick up a card.

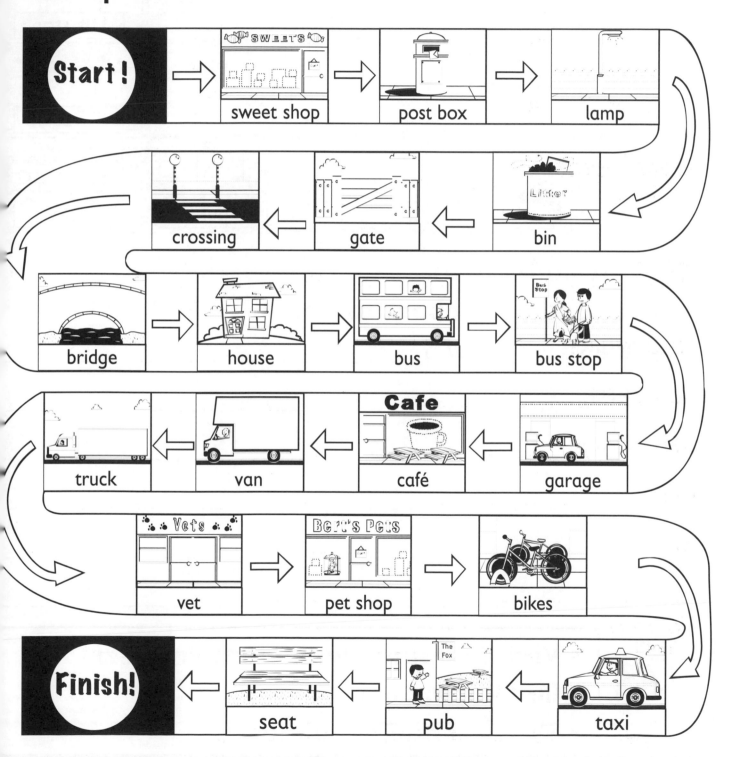

Teachers' note The children will need the cards and the activity from 'Along the street: 2'. Four children can play this dice game. They take turns to roll a dice. They pick up a card (from 'Along the street: 2') according to the items they land on. If they land on an item where the card has already been taken, they move to the next item.

A Lesson for Every Day
Literacy
4–5 Years
© A&C Black

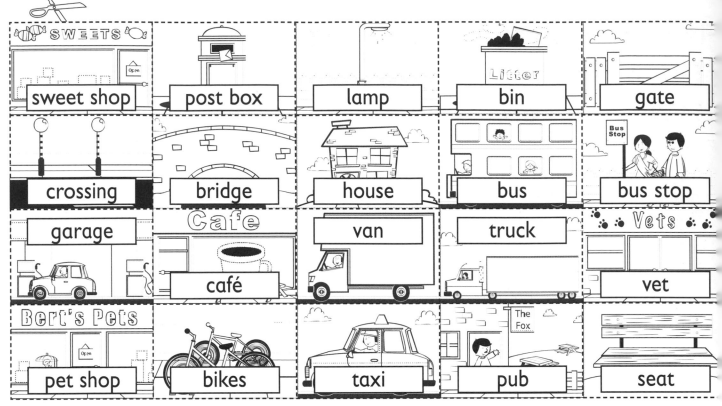

sweet shop	post box	lamp	bin	gate
crossing	bridge	house	bus	bus stop
garage	café	van	truck	vet
pet shop	bikes	taxi	pub	seat

• **Look at your cards.**
• **Write sentences about them.**

Along the street I saw a _____

Then I saw _____

Then I saw _____

Then _____

Then _____

Then _____

NOW TRY THIS!

• **Write about a walk along a street you know.**

Teachers' note This supports the game on 'Along the street: 1'. Once the last player has moved off the board the children should arrange their cards in order. They can then glue them on to a route card and describe the route in sentences, which they could then write, using the format on this page to help them.

A Lesson for Every Day
Literacy
4-5 Years
© A&C Black

I can tap, tap, tap

• Help Teddy to make up a song.
• Do the actions.
• Write the words.

tap

I can _____, _____, _____.

I can _____, _____, _____.

clap

stamp

I can _____, _____, _____.

I can _____, _____, _____.

click

NOW TRY THIS!

What else could Teddy sing?
• **Do the actions.**
• **Sing the song.**
• **Write the words.**

Teachers' note Begin by singing 'I can tap, tap, tap' and tapping your hand on a table top. Repeat this and ask the children to join in. Ask them to look at the next picture and caption and to sing the sentence, and so on. They can then write the missing words.

A Lesson for Every Day
Literacy
4–5 Years
© A&C Black

Old Macdonald's farm

- **What did Old Macdonald have?**
- **Finish the sentences.**

Old Macdonald had a _____.

Old Macdonald had a _____ _____ on that farm he had some _____.

Old Macdonald had a _____ _____ on that _____ he had some _____.

Old Macdonald had a _____ _____ on that _____ he had _____ _____.

Old Macdonald had a _____ _____ on that _____ he had some _____.

NOW TRY THIS!

What else did Old Macdonald have?
- **Sing the song.**
- **Write a sentence.**

Teachers' note Sing the song *Old Macdonald Had a Farm* with the children and then ask them to read the first line. Does it make sense as a sentence? Ask them to supply the missing word and to write it, using the caption to help them to spell it.

A Lesson for Every Day
Literacy
4–5 Years
© A&C Black

Mrs Snip

Make up a song about Mrs Snip.
Finish the sentence.
Write the words.

washes

Mrs Snip _____ my hair.

Splash, splash, splash.

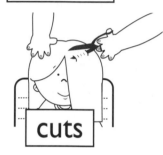

cuts

Mrs Snip _____ my _____.

Snip, _____, _____.

dries

Mrs Snip _____ my hair.

Blow, _____, _____.

combs

Mrs Snip _____ my _____.

Comb, _____, _____.

NOW TRY THIS!

What else could Mrs Snip do?
- **Write a sentence.**
- **Write the words.**

Teachers' note Sing the first line with the children, stopping for them to supply the missing word.
You could sing it to the tune of *Old Macdonald Had a Farm*.) Once they have sung the entire song the
children can write the missing words.

A Lesson for Every Day
Literacy
4–5 Years
© A&C Black

Goldilocks

• **Finish the sentences.**

This is too _____.

hot

This is too _____.

big

This is _____.

small

_____

cold

NOW TRY THIS!

• **Write two other sentences for Goldilocks.**
• **Use the word-bank.**

Word-bank
hard
soft

Teachers' note Ask the children what they know about Goldilocks. What did she do? What did she say? Tell them they are going to read some things Goldilocks said. Invite them to supply the missing words.

A Lesson for Every Day
Literacy
4–5 Years
© A&C Black

Written evidence

Find out about the past from a range of sources

- What types of information could you find out about the past from an old newspaper?

- Design a front page of a newspaper reporting a school event.

Use this idea to help you.

School
New Wildlife area opened

Now try this!
- List three ways a modern newspaper is different from an old-fashioned one.

Teachers' note: Before completing the activity sheet, allow time for the children to examine a selection of different modern newspapers. In small groups children should list what information they contain. Do they all contain the same things? Compare these to old-fashioned newspapers.

16

Photographic evidence

Find out about the past from a range of sources

This photo shows three Victorian children.

Work with a friend.

What can you tell about the children from looking at the photo? _____

What information can you <u>not</u> find out from the photograph? _____

What other evidence could a historian use to find out more about the children? _____

Now try this!
- How are old photos different from modern ones? List your ideas.

Teachers' note: The children should work with partners to discuss their observations and complete the activity sheet. Ask them what they can see in the photo. When was the photo taken? How do they know? Can they be more precise? How old are the children? Can they be sure? What other evidence could they use to find out?

Developing History
Ages 6–7
© A & C BLACK

17

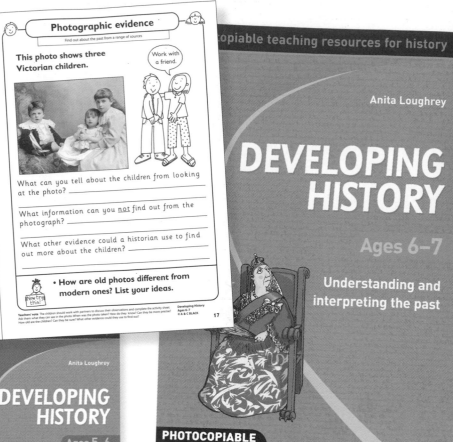

...opiable teaching resources for history

Anita Loughrey

DEVELOPING HISTORY

Ages 6–7

Understanding and interpreting the past

PHOTOCOPIABLE

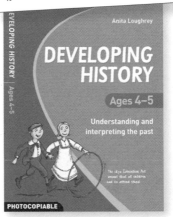

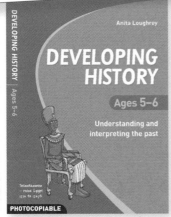

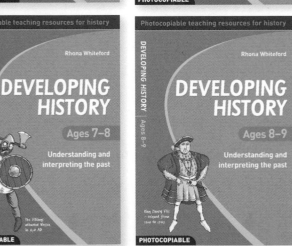

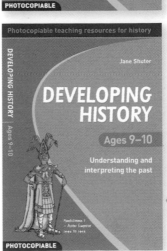

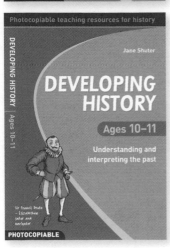

Developing History
Understanding and interpreting the past

A series of 7 photocopiable activity books, helping children to understand and interpret the past through learning about the development of Britain, Europe and the world.

Each book includes:

- Rigorous coverage of the National Curriculum programme of study and the QCA scheme of work for history for the Foundation Stage, Key Stage 1 and Key Stage 2.

- Extension activities to reinforce and develop pupils' learning

- Activities that involve ICT, with links to appropriate websites.

- Teachers' notes that give detailed links to other subjects across the curriculum.

For further information contact
A & C Black Customer Services
Telephone 01256 302 692
Fax 01256 812 521
Or visit our website www.acblack.com